THE

DAY

OF

RUACH

THE THIRD DAY REIGN

Dr. Anita Alexander

Cover and Interior design by Sophie Pauli (www.annasophiadesign.com)

Reach us on the internet: www.revival-flame.org

ISBN 978-0-6485436-4-0

We are truly blessed and fortunate to be alive at this time. Even with all the chaos and uncertainty in this season, opportunities abound all around us! As believers in Yeshua, we have great hope and anticipation of all the Lord will do soon across the earth. Anita Alexander once again delivers a 'now Rhema word' in a masterful, prophetic release and in a truly refreshing way that will open our eyes to our limitless God and cause our Spirits to soar even higher!

The Holy Spirit is moving across the earth in mighty ways. Soon, the Holy RUACH, or breath and wind of His Spirit, will be known by all as our Lord prepares His Body globally for such a demonstration of His power and love invasion that will be evidenced by the saved and yet unsaved in an undeniable way! We each must take our glorious responsibilities as sons of God seriously by pressing into the heart of our Father as never before. The prophets of old dreamed of this day!

Anita is one of the most gifted, anointed, prophetic voices and authors we know in the world today. Anita has written an exquisite, in-depth, and thoroughly Biblically researched treatise that will captivate and enlarge your understanding of revelation and see with the eyes of our Lord the greatest awakening in the largest harvest ever in history. This book is for right now, straight from Abba's heart and throne room at the perfect time in this truly divine set up by the Ancient of Days!

Jorge Parrott, Ph.D.
President of Christ's Mandate for Missions
and the CMM College of Theology
www.cmm.world and www.cmmtheology.org

This is a must-read for our time, and our school will be reading Anita's work. Anita once again captures the heart of the Father with clarity in a tough season as she wields the sword of the Word of God with great skill, knowledge, and revelation. This is a book to be studied and taken to heart. It washes the reader with pure water and renewed hope.

As Anita puts it, she "offers us keys that will educate, empower and equip believers in the preparation process of becoming the sons of God that all of creation is groaning to see."

Nancy G Daniel, Ph.D.
Dean, CMM College of Theology
www.cmmtheology.org

DEDICATION

To the Body of Christ, His beloved, His prize. May intimacy with Christ be the crown jewel, the goal and the mandate for His people, as they behold Him in the beauty of holiness.

CONTENTS

ACKNOWLEDGEMENTS

I would like to acknowledge and honour my mentor and my husband, Sasha Alexander, for truly being my greatest encourager and champion. Thank you for challenging me to go beyond what I believe I am capable of and for leading by example in perseverance, steadfastness and faithfulness to the call of God. Thank you for being my doctrinal sounding board, and for the gentle adjustments and suggestions you input and share that come from decades of studying and pouring over the scriptures. Most importantly, thank you for teaching me how to be a person of the Spirit, and one who is led by the Spirit. Undoubtedly the revelation contained within the pages of this book are built from these very foundations.

Thank you to my children who are all so excited and engaged in all my writing projects. They truly are my cheer squad who delight to see milestones achieved, delightfully offering their congratulations with excited squeals, hugs and high fives upon the completion of the final chapter.

Thank you to Yolande my assistant and editor who truly is my right arm. Your commitment and dedication to seeing me successfully complete this project is wholeheartedly humbling. Thank you.

Thank you to Sophie, once again an outstanding cover design encapsulating the pages within the book. You are such a joy to work with.

FOREWORD

We have entered into a new era, a completely new time in the earth where the Lord is doing a new thing. I remember the day when the Lord spoke the words to me "A new era is coming, and you have not been this way before". I remember the moment when I was surrounded by the call to deep yielded surrender to know His ways, in a way I had not walked in before. It was an invitation to be schooled by the Holy Spirit at a deeper level to know and understand the time we were going to enter into and how to partner with the Lord in all He was going to do.

It was a time to embrace the Refiner's fire and be purified, prepared and positioned for what was coming for us as the people of God. It was a heralding call from the Lord to be "all in" and to "enter in" to the new day that was coming.

In 2017 when I had a dream and the Lord spoke "It's not the end of a season, it's the end of an era", I could hear the sound of bells ringing. I knew that it was the sound of freedom. I knew it was the sound of a company of believers arising on the earth walking in freedom and their authority in ways we had never seen before.

I believe, we have now entered this time in the earth. It is time for His people to govern with Him in the fear of the Lord. It is truly the time to lay aside all "assumptions" and "presumptions" of what we think it should look like, how God should move, and that in the move of God that we will see in this new era, to not attempt to fit it into 'our way' and 'our agenda' and 'boxes'.

It is the time for the overcoming Church (these laid down, surrendered, friends of God, the ones living in adoration of His beauty and Majesty, ministering unto Him, knowing His heart and His ways) to arise in the earth in this new day carrying the blueprint of the Kingdom Government that He is establishing. It is time for those that stand in bold authority with the fire of conviction within them to take the Lord at His Word as His Word is the highest reality and truth.

These ones live from their seat (Ephesians 2:6) and will not move from what He has spoken (knowing He is faithful) and have decided to follow Jesus wherever He leads, however it looks, in radical obedience, to stand for Him, His name and carry His power and Glory.

We have entered the time where the demonstrations of His power, revelation of His Majesty and unveiling of His Glory and the revealing of Jesus Christ in the earth as King and the Lion of Judah, will be unprecedented and He is looking for those who truly know and understand what it looks like to govern with Him.

This incredible book, or should I say gift that has been given to you from the Lord through my faithful friend, Anita Alexander, is a roadmap, a treasure, a sword and a well of revelation for you for this new day, this new era we have entered.

The depth of revelation in these pages is so weighty, it will transform your life and by His Spirit open up to you a whole new realm of spiritual sight to know, discern and understand the days in which we live, and the "Day of Ruach" that is here. These pages contain the meat of His Word in such articulate ways and penned also with such simplicity to understand the times and seasons we have entered and how to navigate these times.

This is not a book to read once and place back on the shelf. This is a MANUAL for this new day. As you read this book you will encounter the Spirit of wisdom and revelation in the knowledge of Him, to awaken you and guide you forth. It will ignite the fire of intimacy within you, the roar of authority through you and a deeper hunger within you to walk in the wisdom of God.

My dear friend Anita Alexander, has been entrusted with such deep and weighty revelation as she lives close to His heart. She lives surrendered, in the fear of the Lord, truly as a friend of God. The purity she carries and the fire of conviction and authority that flows from within her is the conviction and authority that is His ROAR. She is one that understands what it is to govern with her Beloved.

So friend, it is my incredible joy to join with my friend Anita, to welcome you into the journey before you in this book "The Day of Ruach". Take it slow, immerse yourself in the pages and allow the Holy Spirit to speak and minister to you as you read. I know that this journey you're about to embark on, is one that will mark you deeply, encourage you, awaken you, strengthen you and empower you for this new day that is upon us.

Lana Vawser
Lana Vawser Ministries
Author, Speaker, Prophetic Voice
www.lanavawser.com

INTRODUCTION

The prolific signs of the times point us to the closing of this age. Due to the rise of lawlessness and influence of the antichrist spirit which seeks to brainwash a generation into walking a life void of God, there is an overwhelming urgency in this hour to equip believers for the ever-changing and accelerating days at hand. Isaiah 60 declares that gross darkness will cover the earth, however the light of His glory will rise upon His people.

Jesus called those who follow Him sons of the light who are to present the solution to humanity that is swallowed up by darkness. The Lord's mandate for His saints is to invade darkness with the light of His kingdom and to bring in a harvest of souls.

As the closing of this age approaches, this mandate rises to another level of warfare as the enemy seeks to disrupt the times and seasons of God and hold souls captive through his deceptions. The key to victory is for the kingdom of heaven to come on earth.

In 2018 the Lord visited me in a dream announcing the coming "day of the Lord". Prophetically speaking, we stand at the end of this age and scripture clearly reveals the end time church as an overcoming people. It is vital then to understand "how" to overcome and what this signifies from a kingdom perspective, which will enable the Lord's people to step into the timeline of God and successfully flow with this next era in the destiny of His church. The Day of Ruach, is a blueprint of the kingdom government operating in the third day overcoming church.

Chapter 1:

THE DAY OF RUACH

A Dream Of A New Day

It was early hours of the morning August 30th 2018, while I was on a three-day writing retreat that the Lord spoke to me in a dream.

In the dream, I saw a timeline and heard the Lord's voice announce, "THE DAY OF RUACH!" With this sentence came an understanding or a *knowing* that two days had passed, and we now stood at the threshold of entering the "Third Day". Never before had I heard the Lord speak to me using Hebrew words, subsequently confirming that indeed this was a supernatural visitation from the Lord. Even though that day I continued to work on another project, I remained stunned by the weight which these words carried in the dream. I couldn't shake this sentence no matter how hard I tried, which encouraged me to further examine and discover the meaning of the phrase, "the day of ruach". These words seemed relative and imminent, not far away in the distance. My spirit was excited at the thought that these words carried the notion of a new beginning, and thus at the same time prophesying an end. Usually before a beginning arises, an ending occurs.

Unlocking The Mystery

What can be expected of this "new day" or "new beginning" which the Lord proclaimed? How do believers engage in the ongoing preparation season? The first reference point for unpacking and unlocking hidden mysteries in divine encounters and dreams is always the Word of God. Upon waking the Lord quickened to my remembrance Hosea 6:2 (Amplified Classic Version),

> After **two days** He will revive us (quicken us, give us life); on the **third day** He will raise us up that we may live before Him. (emphasis mine)

Following this reference, I was reminded of 2 Peter 3:8 (New King James Version),

> But, beloved, do not forget this one thing, that with the Lord one day is as a thousand years, and a thousand years as one day

Based on the previous scripture, the second and third day from Hosea 6:2 can refer to the number of thousand years. The Lord is clearly disclosing a prophetic timeline where two thousand years have passed since the birth, death and resurrection of Messiah, and where a new era, the *third day,* is about to unfold.

Before further discussing the prophetic timeline in which we now stand, it is important to discover the essence and meaning of the Hebrew word *ruach*. The puzzle pieces of the mystery message delivered in the dream can then converge.

Ruach

It is important to see how the word *ruach* appears in multiple passages of scripture to understand its usage. In order to grasp the foundation and the blueprint regarding the message the Lord was communicating in my dream, let's take a few moments to discover how the word *ruach* has been used in scripture. It is first mentioned in Genesis 1:2-3 (AMPC),

> *The earth was without form and an empty waste, and darkness was upon the face of the very great deep. The **Spirit** of God was moving (hovering, brooding) over the face of the waters. And God said, "Let there be light"; and there was light. (emphasis mine)*

The Amplified Classic Version has chosen to translate *ruach* in Genesis 1:2-3 as *Spirit*.

The Strong's concordance defines the Hebrew word *ruach* as: *wind, breath, spirit, a sense of violent exhalation, courage, anger, whirlwind.*[1]

The *ruach* of God or as the Hebrew reads in this particular scripture, *Ruach Elohiym* - the Spirit *of* God, is the creator of the universe, and all mankind.[2] This is the first connotation of *by His Spirit*. It was *by His Spirit* He created. This first mention of *ruach* in scripture reveals the blueprint of how the Lord operates and how His people who are created in *His likeness* are designed to function (Genesis 1:27).

The "Day of Ruach" therefore pronounces the day of His people operating *by His Spirit*.

---

[1]   James Strong, Strong's Expanded Exhaustive Concordance of the Bible
       (Nashville: Thomas Nelson, 2009), s.v. "*Ruach*"
[2]   Ibid., "*elohiym*"

In Romans 8:14, Paul explains that all who are led by the Spirit of God are the sons of God. Further down in verse 19, he proceeds to elaborate and disclose that the whole of creation has been groaning in pains of labour for the full manifestation of the sons of God. So in essence, all creation has been waiting for the revealing of those who will be led and function *by His Spirit.*

As I began to understand what the Lord was showing me regarding the coming forth of the sons of God, He reminded me of an encounter I had with Him in worship years before I had this dream. In the encounter I saw a vision of the four faced cherubim mentioned in Ezekiel 1. The four faces kept revolving before my eyes, interchanging between the ox, the eagle, the lion and the man. This went on for a short period until suddenly the switching of each face stopped and I found myself staring into the face of the man. I heard the Lord say as this happened, "These days now coming will see the sons of God revealed."

Let us continue with our short study on the *ruach* to discern and interpret my dream.

In Genesis 1:3, *ruach* is used in conjunction with the word Elohim, meaning the Spirit *of* God, that is like breath or wind. In other scriptures the word *ruach* is simply mentioned as wind, with no attachment to the *person* or the *Spirit of* God. A viable example is found in Proverbs 25:14 (King James Version);

> *Whoso boasteth himself of a false gift is like clouds and wind (root Hebrew word ruach), without rain. (emphasis mine)*

In this scripture it would be incorrect to interpret the word *ruach* as the "Spirit of God". If so, it would read as; Whoso boasteth himself of a false gift is like clouds and the *Spirit of God* without rain.

Evidently, this does not make sense. Therefore, when unlocking mysteries and interpreting prophetic revelations in dreams and visions, it is essential to unravel the context of the given disclosure, comparably to how bible translators examine the framework of the Hebrew text. According to the Strong's concordance, the word *ruach* is also used separately from the *person* of God.

Further uses of *ruach* in scripture have been utilized to explain and reveal the *force* and *power* of God.

It was also by the *ruach* of God that Israel saw a mighty deliverance from the captivity of Egypt.

Exodus 15:8-10 (KJV)

> *And with the **blast** of thy nostrils the waters were gathered together, the floods stood upright as a heap, and the depths were congealed in the heart of the sea. The enemy said, I will pursue, I will overtake, I will divide the spoil; my lust shall be satisfied upon them; I will draw my sword, my hand shall destroy them. Thou didst blow thy **wind**, the sea covered them; they sank as lead in the mighty waters. (emphasis mine)*

As mentioned in verse 8 of the scripture above, The King James Version translates the Hebrew word *ruach* as blast.[3] In other words, the wind (*ruach*) blown from His nostrils was with such violent force that it caused the waters of the red sea to stand upright so the children of Israel could pass onto the other side. In verse ten, *ruach* is translated as wind that closed the sea upon the Egyptians.[4]

In this example the *ruach* is the *force* and *power* of God that brings deliverance, makes a way where there is no way, and it is also the force that defeats the enemy on behalf of His people. It is the *hand* of God that performs in the measure of His unseen breath, His wind and His force.

---

3   James Strong, Strong's Expanded Exhaustive Concordance of the Bible (Nashville: Thomas Nelson, 2009), s.v. "*blast*".

4   Ibid., "*wind*"

Other words used to interpret the Hebrew word *ruach* according to Brown-Driver-Briggs Lexicon are energy of life and vital power.[5] The term "vital power" can be explained as a force. The *ruach* of God is the *force* that demonstrates and executes his intent, will and purpose.

Vriezen explains in his article "*Ruach Yahweh (Elohim) in the Old Testament*", that the *ruach* of God fills or comes upon a person, for the purpose of accomplishing their God-given task. He adds, "*It makes those who are called into perfect instruments in the hands of Yahweh, one might perhaps say, into an extension of God in this world.*"[6]

One could say that is exactly what sonship is, an extension of God on this earth.

The third day which the Lord titled as the "The Day of Ruach" will involve an unveiling of the sons of God operating *by the Spirit* and demonstrating the unprecedented force and power of God.

Knowing that *ruach* is interpreted differently throughout scripture, it is clear that the Lord in my dream was referring to *ruach* in the context of *His Spirit* and the *force* and *power* thereof instead of the natural wind or breath.

The Third Day And The Prophetic Week

The second connotation of the dream is that two days had passed and we were entering the *third day*, "The Day of Ruach". As I mentioned earlier, the scripture the Lord first brought to my attention when praying over my dream was Hosea 6:2 (AMPC);

> *After two days, He will revive us (quicken us, give us life); on the third day He will raise us up that we may live before Him.*

---

5   Enhanced Brown-Driver-Briggs Hebrew and English Lexicon, Clarendon Press, 1977 "*Ruach*"

6   Th. C. Vriezen, "Ruach Yahweh (Elohim) in the Old Testament", Neotestamentica Issue#1, Jan 1966:51

As explained earlier, 2 Peter 3:8 (NKJV) defines the meaning of these days in light of the Lord's timeline.

> *But, beloved, do not forget this one thing, that with the Lord one day is as a thousand years, and a thousand years as one day.*

In the opening chapter of the *"Army of the Dawn"*, Rick Joyner begins to describe the biblical "prophetic week" by explaining how the genealogies in scripture reveal the biblical timeline over a period of seven thousand years. When we look at 2 Peter 3:8 concerning the Lord's duration of a day, a thousand years can be seen as a prophetic day. According to Joyner, the genealogies starting from Adam add up to around six thousand years, thus nearly approaching the seventh prophetic day. He refers to the Book of Barnabus 13:2-5 where the concept of this prophetic biblical week is deciphered based on the seven days of creation. It furthermore suggests that all things will be accomplished within this six-day period (six thousand years) and confirms the return of Christ on the seventh day. Joyner shows that Matthew 12:8 *For the Son of Man is Lord even of the Sabbath*, refers to the seventh day of the prophetic biblical week.[7]

This seventh day is also referenced by many biblical teachers as the millennial "Reign with Christ" (Revelation 20:4-6). Dr. Lester Sumrall expounds further on this understanding of the "prophetic week" in his book *"The Millennial Reign of Christ"*. He states that the Thursday and Friday of the prophetic week correspond with the period commencing from the resurrection of Christ until the present moment and that it is currently Friday night. He continues to describe this seventh day as the time when the saints will enter the kingdom age, the messianic millennial rule and reign with Christ over the nations.[8]

---

7   Joyner, Army of the Dawn. 8,9
8   Sumrall, The Millennial Reign of Christ (Indianna: LeSEA
       Publishing, 2009),4.

Based on these explanations of the *prophetic week*, the seventh day or the Sabbath is equivalent to the *third day* mentioned in Hosea 6:2.

According to the timeline of the ages, it is now the end of the *second day*. Two thousand years have passed since the death, burial and resurrection of Messiah Jesus Christ and the people of God / Bride of Christ, are being prepared to enter this *third day*.

When studying Hosea 6:2-3 in more depth, there is still additional revelation to unfold.

> *After two days, He will revive us (quicken us, give us life); on the third day He will raise us up that we may live before Him. Yes let us know (recognise, be acquainted with, and understand) Him; let us be zealous to know the Lord [to appreciate, give heed to, and cherish Him]. His going forth is prepared and certain as the dawn, and He will come to us as the [heavy] rain, as the latter rain that waters the earth.*

According to this passage there are some events that are going to take place *before* the third day and *after* the second. Hosea notes that the Lord will revive His people after two days, which is a period of preparation or transition. I believe that we are in that window now, before stepping into the third day.

Verse 2b of Hosea 6 says,

> *on the third day He will **raise** us up that we may **live before Him.** (emphasis mine)*

Some Hebrew translations of the word *raise up* according to Brown-Driver-Briggs are: to rise, establish, confirm, to fulfil, to be proven, to be made valid, to make stand up.[9]

---

9   Enhanced Brown-Driver-Briggs Hebrew and English Lexicon, Clarendon Press, 1977 *"raise"*

Raise up is used numerous times in scripture where the Lord addresses "the establishing of His covenant" (Genesis 6:18, Genesis 9:9, Genesis 9:11, Genesis 17:7, Genesis 17:19, Leviticus 26:9, Deuteronomy 8:18). To establish means; to make it valid, causing it to stand.

The Hebrew word for *live* according to the Strong's Concordance is *chavah* signifying to revive, the same Hebrew word utilized in the verse above.[10]

Brown-Driver-Briggs' definition describes *chayah* as: to sustain life, remain alive, to have life, to be alive.[11]

The Hebrew interpretation for *before Him* according to the Strong's Concordance is *paniym*, which translates as: the face or the very presence of the Lord.[12]

Hosea 6:2, therefore, displays the *third day* as the period where the Lord's bride is equipped, established, fixed and secure without wavering or backsliding in her covenant with Him. She is a people who remains alive and sustained in and by His presence, will carry the governmental rights to execute that covenant on this earth.

Prophetic Symbolism Of The Third Day

The wedding at Cana, a prophetic picture of the third day Church.

John 2:1-10

> *On the **third day** there was a wedding at Cana of Galilee, and the mother of Jesus was there. Jesus also was invited*

---

10   James Strong, Strong's Expanded Exhaustive Concordance of the Bible
        (Nashville: Thomas Nelson, 2009), s.v. "*live*"
11   Enhanced Brown-Driver-Briggs Hebrew and English Lexicon,
        Clarendon Press, 1977 "*live*"
12   James Strong, Strong's Expanded Exhaustive Concordance of the Bible
        (Nashville: Thomas Nelson, 2009), s.v. "*before Him*"

with His disciples to the wedding. And when the wine was all gone, the mother of Jesus said to Him, they have no wine! Jesus said to her, Woman, what is that to you and to me? My time (hour to act) has not yet come. His mother said to the servants, Whatever He says to you, do it. Now there were six water pots of stone standing there, as the Jewish custom of purification (ceremonial washing) demanded, holding twenty to thirty gallons a piece. Jesus said to them, fill the water pots with water. So they filled them up to the brim. Then He said to them, draw some out now and take it to the manager of the feast. So they took him some. And when the manager tasted the water just now turned into wine, not knowing where it came from - though the servants who had drawn the water knew - he called the bridegroom. And said to him, everyone else serves his best wine first, then he serves that which is not so good; but you have kept back the good wine until now! (emphasis mine)

Who has ever noticed that the wedding of Cana was on the *third* day? The Lord loves to hide hints throughout the scriptures and every detail is in there for a reason. Many have interpreted the wedding at Cana as a symbolic picture of the Lord (the bridegroom) saving the best "wine" for His end time bride, the church.

Wine is commonly representative of the outpouring of the Holy Spirit and the glory of God. Ephesians 5:18 says; *Do not get drunk with wine, for that is debauchery; but ever be filled and stimulated with the Holy Spirit.* This verse indicates a correlation between the Spirit of God and wine.

In Acts 2:15-17, on the *third* hour of the day of Pentecost, Peter reflecting a state of drunkenness, boldly declared the words of the prophet Joel. He explained he was not drunk with wine, but that this was the beginning of the end time outpouring of God's Spirit. Not by coincidence, but again pointing to the end time outpouring of the glory and power of God upon His prepared people.

Another prophetic allegory mentioning three days, is found in Joshua 3:1-5, where the children of Israel were about to cross over into the promised land.

> *Joshua rose early in the morning and they removed from Shittim and came to the Jordan, he and all the Israelites, and lodged there before passing over. After* **three** *days the officers went through the camp, Commanding the people: When you see the ark of the covenant of the Lord your God being borne by the Levitical priests, set out from where you are and follow it. Yet a space must be kept between you and it, about 2,000 cubits by measure: come not near it, that you may [be able to see the ark and] know the way you must go, for you have not passed this way before. And Joshua said to the people, Sanctify yourselves [that is, separate yourselves for a special holy purpose], for tomorrow* **the Lord will do wonders among you.** *(emphasis mine)*

Hebrews 3:19 refers to the promised land as the "Lord's rest". This, as we discussed earlier, is the sabbath (seventh) day on the prophetic week. Thus, as we read in the verse above, in preparation for the children of Israel to cross over in the Lord's rest and "inherit" their promise, they camped before the Jordan for *three days* and were instructed to sanctify themselves as the Lord was going to perform wonders among them. Furthermore, the instruction was to follow the ark (the presence of God) and make sure they could "see" it as they had not passed that way before. This whole scenario prophesies that we, the latter day church must sanctify ourselves in order to enter into the promised land, the Lord's millennial reign of the "Third Day" (the seventh day of the sabbath rest where the Lord will do 'wonders' among us).

The word "sanctify" can also be translated as consecrate, which means set apart. In the next chapter we will delve further into the necessity and meaning of this process in order to step into the Third Day.

Furthermore, being *led by the Spirit* (following the ark) is also essential for crossing over into the promise of God, His rest, as we His people have never been this "way" before.

In essence, sense and reason, man's carnal ways and ideas, will not empower the church to step into the "Third Day", the "The Day of Ruach". But a people prepared and made ready (consecrated and sanctified), being able to be led by the Spirit of God, will surely be in place for this victorious closing of the ages.

Resurrection Power Will Mark The Third Day Church

Hosea 6:3 unlocks further revelation regarding the term "Day of Ruach".

> *Yes let us know (recognize, be acquainted with, and understand) Him; let us be zealous to know the Lord [to appreciate, give heed to, and cherish Him]. His going forth is prepared and certain as the dawn, and **He will come to us as the [heavy] rain, as the latter rain** that waters the earth. (emphasis mine)*

The Lord reveals here that His "going forth" is as certain as the sunrise. In other words, He is stating that He will do that which He said He would do. He, furthermore, communicates that He is going to come as the latter rain. Rain often appears throughout scripture as a metaphorical expression of the outpouring of His Spirit and the blessings and favour of the Lord (Lev 26:4, Acts 14:17, Joel 2:23).

Hosea 6:3 describes the *type* of rain, namely a *latter* rain, which speaks of the last rain before harvest, also known as a "downpour flooding". Prophetically, this represents the last outpouring of God's Spirit upon His prepared saints before the harvest of souls at the end of the age.

Haggai 2:9 declares that the latter glory of the second temple will far exceed that of the former (the former referring to Solomon's temple). This ultimately portrays that though the second temple's natural beauty did not come close to that of Solomon's original masterpiece, the Lord was promising to adorn it with Himself and His glory in a greater fashion than ever before. The Old Testament is known as a prophetic allegory of the New Testament; therefore, it is assumed the Lord is referring to the former and latter house of the New Covenant. God's people are now His temple (1 Corinthians 6:19) and the glory of the Lord is no longer housed in brick and mortar as in the old temple. The former and latter houses correspond, respectively, to the early church born at the time of Jesus, and the end time church in this day and age.

It is interesting to note that at two different times the Jews and Pharisees asked Jesus for a sign to prove He was authorized, sent from heaven and He was who He said He was. In both instances he responded with a *third day* allegory.

John 2:18-21

> *Then the Jews retorted, what sign can you show us, seeing You do these things? [What sign, miracle, token, indication can You give us as evidence that You have authority and are commissioned to act in this way?] Jesus answered them, destroy (undo) this temple, and in* **three days** *I will raise it up again. Then the Jews replied, it took forty-six years to build this temple (sanctuary), and will You raise it up in three days? But He had spoken of the temple which was His body. (emphasis mine)*

The temple is used here as a metaphor for the Lord's body. He was prophetically articulating that He would rise from death on the third day in the same way His end time church will rise in resurrection power to overcome victoriously.

The second example of Jesus replying with a third day analogy is found in Matthew 12:38-40,

> *Then some of the scribes and Pharisees said to Him, Teacher, we desire to see a sign or miracle from You [proving that You are what You claim to be]. But He replied to them, an evil and adulterous generation (a generation morally unfaithful to God) seeks and demands a sign; but no sign shall be given to it except the sign of the prophet Jonah. For even as Jonah was **three days** and three nights in the belly of the sea monster, so will the Son of Man be three days and three nights in the heart of the earth. (emphasis mine)*

Again Jesus' answer to certify His identity was the sign of Jonah, not in reference to Nineveh's repentance but to the three days spent in the whale's belly. These two examples of Jesus' response indicated the manifestation of resurrection power on the third day which validated and confirmed that He was sent from heaven. Confidently knowing this to be true, the same will *validate* His end time Church as ones sent from the Lord.

Rick Joyner mentions in *"The Call"* that Jonah was endowed with the greatest power of prophetic oration in the history of mankind. He believes this mantle of powerful preaching will be gifted to the bride in the last days. Even the most wicked, will repent and turn to the King of Heaven.[13]

Maybe that is why the evil citizens of Nineveh turned from their wicked hard-hearted ways and repented sincerely before the Lord. Could it be that Jonah was walking in a latter glory, prophesying the ages to come?

The writers of "One for Israel" note in their article "The Former and Latter Rains in Israel", that Joel 2:23 ESV *(Be glad, O children of Zion, and rejoice in the Lord your God, for he has given the early rain for your **vindication**;*

---

13   Joyner, The Call, 52-53.

he has poured down for you abundant rain, the early and the latter rain, as before), depicts the early and latter rains as outpourings of the Spirit of God vindicating the ministries of His people. The authors further surmise that the miracles and demonstrations of God's awesome power, accompanying the early church and validating their message, will reoccur at the end of the age, but in greater measure likened to the flooding latter rains.[14]

With this in sight, it is viable to conclude that a clear "sign" of the third day church will be a people walking in resurrection, governmental power able to undo and overthrow ancient demonic strongholds over nations/peoples and deliver the righteousness and justice of freedom purchased at the cross of Calvary.

The Third Day Blueprint – The Overcomer Governing *By His Spirit*

Zechariah 4:6 is a famous scripture many quote in relation to the power of God accomplishing that which man cannot. It, however, is crucial to consider the context by which this scripture was declared. This was in reference to the finishing of the second temple. The people encountered a lot of opposition and resistance when building this temple. After a series of interferences and obstacles, Zechariah finally proclaimed to Zerubbabel the governor and prince of Judah *"Not by might, nor by power, but by My Spirit", says the Lord."*

The Hebrew word for Spirit here is *ruach!* Zechariah pronounced further in verse 7 that because it will be done *by His Spirit*, all the mountains of human obstacles and opposition will be made a flat plain before them. Zerubbabel would indeed be granted the power to fulfil that which he had started and would surely bring forth the finishing stone with loud shouts of grace, grace.

---

14   "The Former and Latter Rains in Israel", oneforisrael.org, May 17, 2016,
        www.oneforisrael.org/amp/bible-based-teaching-from-israel/the-former-latter-rains-in-israel

After unpacking the context behind Zechariah 4:6, a prophetic blueprint is displayed concerning the latter day house accomplishing all *by His Spirit*, indeed bringing forth the finishing stone, the closing of the ages, ushering in the third day, the "Day of Ruach", the Day of the Lord's power, a third day church governing in resurrection power where all human and demonic obstacles will be made a flat plain.

All things will be restored as His people operate *by His Spirit* and *in His likeness* as first laid out in Genesis 1:2, 3, 26. This will mark the fulfilment of the ages, as the sons of God come forth shining in the light and glory of God.

Chapter 2:

THE END OF THE SECOND DAY – A RETURN TO GOVERNMENTAL FOUNDATIONS

Receiving The Blueprint Of Government

A key to note in the sentence the Lord spoke to me in the dream was the connotation of *entering* the third day. This word carries an implication of transition rather than arrival. The Lord was prophetically announcing His Bride transitioning from one era into another. Most transitions involve an ending of the old season and a time of preparation for the new.

As previously stated, the third day signifies the seventh day of the prophetic week or the millennial reign with Christ. The *kingdom age* will be a time where the people of God step into their allotted governmental positions. *Rule* is a governmental word which implies authority. Hence, the *third day* is the governmental mantling of the saints who have first been revived and have "made themselves" ready.

Revelation 19:7 (English Standard Version),

> *Let us rejoice and exult and give him the glory, for the marriage*
> *of the Lamb has come, and his Bride has made herself ready;*

As the day of ruling and reigning with Christ approaches, it is essential to comprehend the preparation process of His Bride at the end of the *second* day. The Lord announcing the "Day of Ruach" is an invitation from heaven to all believers with ears to hear what the Spirit of the Lord is saying, to apprehend and engage in a season of preparation that would ultimately enable them to successfully step into the new day.

He is releasing the blueprint of government in this hour, allowing time for His people to prepare themselves for this glorious promotion coming. This third day church will rule and reign in resurrection power. But how do God's people, young and old, mature or just born again, begin to comprehend the finer details of how and what that looks like? How to govern with Christ? How to overcome? How to make oneself ready?

After Two Days He Will REVIVE Us

What an honour to have a heavenly Father who is tireless in His pursuit to restore His sons and daughters into intimate relationship with Him. Throughout the generations from Genesis to Revelation, scripture is filled with countless records of the Lord's pursuit of intimate relationship with mankind. In His genius and flawless display of fatherly love, a way was made for His children to be reconciled into His bosom through our Lord Jesus Christ. The main purpose of covenant is to restore mankind back to original or initial position at creation, namely the ability to operate *in His likeness, by His Spirit.*

The next three chapters will delve into discovering the events that need to take place at the end of the second day in order for the Lord's people to successfully enter the third day explained by the prophet Hosea.

Hosea 6:2 (NKJV)

> *After two days He will **revive** us; On the third day He will raise us up, that we may live in His sight. (emphasis mine)*

By uncovering the deeper meanings and synonyms of *revive,* it delivers a greater ability to see and grasp the picture Hosea was seeking to present to His audience in regards to what would be taking place at the end of the *second* day.

As mentioned in the first chapter, the Hebrew word for *revive* according to the Strong's Concordance is *Chayah.*

It means: to revive, give life, restore to life, save, be whole, preserve, quicken, recover, make alive.[15]

According to the Merriam Webster dictionary, some meanings for the word *revive* are: to restore to life or consciousness, to become active or flourishing again, to restore from a depressed, inactive, or unused state, to bring back, to renew in the mind or memory

Synonyms of "revive" include:

Resuscitate   – bring back from the edge of death, bring someone (back) to their senses

Rekindle   – to begin to burn again, to start or stir something up

Awake   – bring out of a sleeping state

Resurrect   – to raise from the dead[16]

This period of reviving will announce the closing of the second day as the verse specifies (***after*** two days). *Revive* is clearly not referring to the third

---

15   James Strong, Strong's Expanded Exhaustive Concordance of the Bible (Nashville: Thomas Nelson, 2009), s.v. *"revive"*

16   *Merriam-Webster.com Dictionary,* s.v. "revive", accessed November 10, 2020, www.merriam-webster.com/dictionary/revive.

day, because what takes place on the third day is expressed in the next part of the verse. Therefore, it is valid to conclude that this "reviving" occurs in the transition phase *between* the second and third day which is where the church is at now.

Thus Hosea 6:2 reveals that *after* the second day His people are in need of reviving. It is plausible to determine that at the closing of the second day, the church is asleep, spiritually dead, their love for God has waxed cold and is not on fire, they are nearing the edge of death, unconscious, inactive, depressed, in need of saving, restoring and recovering, (obviously a spiritual state of death, not a natural one). Moreover as the Hebrew explains their mind and memory needs restoring in the knowledge of who they are.

This raises the following questions. Why are God's people in this state? Why are they dysfunctional, inactive and depressed? Why has their love for God grown cold and have they fallen asleep? Why are they near the edge of death and in need of restoring and saving? The answer is found in the verse below.

Hosea 6:1

> *Come and let us **return to the Lord**, for He has torn so that*
> *He may heal us; He has stricken so that He may bind us up.*
> *(emphasis mine)*

Hosea is calling the people of God to return to the Lord, indicating they have strayed and are not walking with Him. This plea to return exhibits a people who have deviated from their life source and broken *covenant* with their God, which is the main reason why they need reviving.

The early church operated in the power and glory of the new covenant delivered through Jesus' sacrifice. Peter's shadow healed people, Philip translated, Stephen shone with the glory of God as he was martyred, Paul was bitten by a poisonous snake and lived, the apostle John was unable to be boiled in oil and so on. So, what has happened since then until now? Man is what happened; mixture crept in. Paul was continually cautioning the early church to protect the purity of the gospel they preached. Galatians chapter 1 and 3, 1 Corinthians 11 and 2 Timothy 4:3-4 are just a few mentions of Paul's admonitions to the early church of how the enemy would continually seek to pollute the truth. This pollution sought to bring man back into self-righteousness which ultimately defers glory unto man rather than God. Another word for this is religion.

Religion substitutes relationship and intimacy with God with external deeds of righteousness, imposing a new "standard" rooted in the carnality of man's wisdom. This is what Paul boldly addressed with the Galatian church in Galatians chapter 3, posing the question who had BEWITCHED them out of being led by the spirit and back into striving for perfection by dependence on the flesh. As soon as this pollution takes root, God's people are led away from His "presence", therefore, no longer eating from the tree of life, but from the tree of the knowledge of good and evil. This ploy to render the church of God powerless was the enemy's quest in the garden of Eden and since the birth of the early church, slowly but surely deceiving God's people back into dead works of religion and seeking power and righteousness apart from God. In this space, their identity is lost, they forget who they are and whose they are. This then results in a spiritual "death", a "falling asleep" in which an awakening is needed to bring His beloved back into the presence of God, eating from the tree of life, and walking in the fullness of identity and dominion.

It is evident since the birth of the early church over these last two thousand years that this work and strategy of the enemy has succeeded to a great extent. For this reason, we now stand at the end of the second day with His people, His beloved, in need of reviving, recalling who they are and whose they are and being raised from spiritual death to their spiritual senses.

The true governmental authority that Jesus restored has been lost through religion. Jesus gave us the keys to the kingdom, which represent governmental authority but through religion man has misplaced the keys. In the reviving process at the end of the second day, the Lord is returning His people back to governmental authority by causing them to rediscover the keys of the kingdom He already gave them two thousand years ago.

Understanding Covenant

The word *"covenant"* is of Latin origin (*con venire*), meaning a coming together. It presupposes two or more parties who come together to make a contract, agreeing on promises, stipulations, privileges, and responsibilities.[17]

Covenant is relationship language. Nowadays the word is more commonly heard when referring to relationships such as marriage. In ancient times it was used in reference to how nations conducted their relationships with each other. Thus, it is a relationship agreement between two parties based on promises and responsibilities, or in other words a pledge of allegiance.

Jeremiah prophesied the picture of the New Covenant, which the church is part of through Jesus Christ.

Jeremiah 31:31-34 (NKJV)

> *Behold the days are coming, says the Lord, when I will make a new covenant with the house of Israel and with the house of Judah - not according to the covenant that I made with their fathers in the day that I took them by the hand to lead them out of the land of Egypt, My covenant which they broke, though I was a husband to them, says the Lord. But this is the covenant which I will make with the house of Israel after those days, says the Lord: I will put My law in their minds, and write it on their hearts; and I will be their God, and they shall be My people. No more shall every man teach his neighbor, and every man his brother, saying, "know the*

---

17   "What is a Covenant?-Biblical meaning and Importance today", Christianity.com, April 17, 2019, www.christianity.com/wiki/bible/what-is-a-covenant-biblical-meaning-and-importance-today.html

Lord," for they all shall know Me, from the least of them to
the greatest of them, says the Lord. For I will forgive their
iniquity, and their sin I will remember no more.

The Lord is exposing an allegory of His covenant with Israel by presenting Himself as Israel's husband. This concept continues in the New Covenant based on the sacrifice of Jesus Christ. We are His bride and He is the bridegroom (John 3:29, Mark 2:19, Matthew 25, Revelation 22:17). The first mention of man and wife coming into covenant was explained in Genesis 2:24 (NKJV),

Therefore a man shall leave his father and mother and be
joined to his wife, and they shall become one flesh.

The picture portrayed here is union, becoming one. God desires union. He seeks that His people would unite with Him, in every facet of their being. According to the New Covenant ratified in the blood of Jesus Christ, man has been granted the ability to become one with the Lord via the Holy Spirit. When a believer is born again, according to 2 Corinthians 5:17-20 they are now a new creation, the old has gone and they have been reconciled unto God through Him who knew no sin and became sin for them that they might become the righteousness of God.

If then from God's point of view, covenant with His people, according to the Old and New Testaments, is seen and prized the same as a marriage covenant between man and wife, it simplifies it for the church to understand and grasp the expectations surrounding this covenant. Someone determining the principal condition of a marriage covenant would most likely state something as 'loyalty, monogamy and faithfulness for the entirety of one's married life'. In Matthew 5:27-28, 32, Jesus points out that the very act that breaks a marriage covenant is infidelity in deed or thought. Loyalty and faithfulness at the opposite end of the spectrum maintain a marriage covenant as both parties declare their life long devotion and monogamy to each other. This is parallel to a covenant with God. He desires union through loyalty and allegiance. The new commandment has not changed. God's people are to love the Lord with all their heart, soul and will, signifying they are His completely, having no other gods before Him.

Mark 12:29-31 (NKJV)

> *Jesus answered him, "The first of all the commandments is: "Hear, o Israel, the Lord our God, the Lord is one. And you shall love the Lord your God with all your heart, with all your soul, with all your mind, and with all your strength." This is the first commandment. And the second, like it, is this: "You shall love your neighbor as yourself." There is no other commandment greater than these.*

John Piper in His article *"The New Covenant and the New Covenant People"*, explains that the two issues that separate man and God in their relationship are solved in the New Covenant.

1. The guilt of sin, resolved through Jesus' shedding of blood that removed the shame and guilt of humanity by taking it upon Himself.

2. Rebellion, purged because of His law written on the heart of man, resulting in a union between God and man's will.[18]

Along with Jeremiah, this is also confirmed by the prophet Ezekiel.

Ezekiel 36:26-29a (NKJV)

> *I will give you a new heart and put a new spirit within you; I will take the heart of stone out of your flesh and give you a heart of flesh. I will put My Spirit within you and **cause you to walk in My statutes, and you will keep My judgments and do them.** Then you shall dwell in the land that I gave to your*

---

18   John Piper, "The New Covenant and the New Covenant People", desiringgod.org, February 7, 1993, www.desiringgod.org/messages/the-new-covenant-and-the-new-covenant-people

fathers; you shall be My people, and I will be your God. I will **deliver you from all your uncleanness**.... *(emphasis mine)*

In a covenant relationship the Lord requires obedience to His ways, allegiance to His leadership and consecration through sanctification.

Those in a New Covenant relationship, who are filled with the Spirit and have the Law of God written upon their hearts, are a people able to walk obediently in the statutes of God.

The New Covenant signifies obedience, allegiance and consecration, which is contrary to some new age doctrines that have infiltrated the Body of Christ in recent decades, sprouting heresies that the New Covenant is a licence to sin without consequence. Hebrews 10:26-27 teaches that those who wilfully and deliberately sin after having acquired the knowledge of the truth, position themselves for divine judgement as ones who set themselves in opposition to God! Verse 29 expounds that they will encounter a worse judgement and those that consider the blood covenant of Jesus Christ by which one has been consecrated as common and unholy, display the insulting act of trampling the Son of God under foot! God's desired outcome has not changed, the New Covenant is not a licence to sin but rather the access to God's grace, empowering us, His people, to overcome the carnal nature that keeps us in bondage to sin and prevents an intimate relationship with God.

Romans 8:11 (NKJV)

But if the Spirit of Him who raised Jesus from the dead dwells in you, He who raised Christ from the dead will also give life to your mortal bodies through His Spirit who dwells within you.

This same Spirit that raised Christ from the dead is the same Spirit that dwells in us and helps us overcome the mortality of our carnal beings. In other words, His spirit dwelling within, empowers His people to stay in covenant through obedience and allegiance to Him by overcoming and subduing the sinful nature that is inherently in rebellion to God. The law of Moses was expectation without Holy Spirit empowerment, as man was unable to remain loyal due to the fallen nature. The New Covenant offers empowerment by the *grace* of God being accessible through the cleansing and remission of sins. Mankind is unable to be obedient in its own strength and based on its own merits. It is by the infilling of the Holy Spirit and the Law being inscribed upon our hearts, that we are enabled to be led by the Spirit and not fulfil the dictates of the flesh. We, His saints, are able to live in unbroken fellowship with Him through the blood of Christ that cleanses us from all unrighteousness.

Faith – The Foundation Of Covenant

The Lord made covenant with Abraham, the original patriarch of Israel. In this covenant, God promised him and his seed, that they would be a nation belonging to God under His protection and through his descendants all the nations of the earth would be blessed (Genesis 12, 15, 17). Paul explains in Galatians 3, that this covenant with Abraham was based on faith not Law. Christ purchased freedom and redeemed His people from the curse of the Law (being that man cannot fulfil it by his own strength) by becoming a curse. Therefore, through receiving Christ Jesus, the blessing promised to Abraham could now come to the Gentiles as well as the Jewish people, through faith, all having the opportunity to receive the promise of the Holy Spirit. There is now no distinction between Jew nor Greek, but those belonging to Christ (who is Abraham's seed) are Abraham's offspring and spiritual heirs according to the promise.

The foundation of this spiritual inheritance is through the covenant of Abraham, which was a covenant of faith not Law. Galatians 3:12 instructs that the Law does not rest on faith and has nothing to do with faith. The apostle Paul teaches in Galatians 3 that the covenant made with Abraham was based on virtue of a promise. The purpose of the Law was to disclose to man his incapability of keeping covenant in his own strength and thus was in need of a saviour. Man needed "help" to keep covenant, to walk with God and to remain as God's own. This help is the promise of the Holy Spirit. Ephesians 2:8 states that it is *"by grace through faith we are saved and partakers of Christ's salvation"*. Therefore, the promises of the covenant God made with Abraham are received and accessed via the same foundation it was established on, namely by grace through faith. Everything Christ has redeemed for His people is obtained by faith.

New Covenant Enables Governmental Access

Ephesians 2:6 reveals that part of the promise of the New Covenant in Christ is we have been given a joint seating with Him in the heavenly sphere. Meaning, we have been raised to the same governmental position as Jesus and have been given access to the same authority God has given Him. So in order to access and walk in kingdom governmental rights we must understand this is through walking in covenant. Faith is the key component in the covenant with God, and the ability to walk in the kingdom governmental authority available to believers.

The Sign Of A Covenant People

When God made covenant with Abraham, He commanded every male among him to be circumcised as an outward sign or token of keeping covenant with God.

Genesis 17:10-11

> *This is My covenant, which you shall keep, between Me and you and your posterity after you: Every male among you shall be circumcised. And you shall circumcise the flesh of your foreskin, and it shall be a token or sign of the covenant (the promise or pledge) between Me and you.*

In Deuteronomy 30:6 this symbolic act of circumcision is realized;

And the Lord your God will circumcise your hearts and the hearts of your descendants, **to love the Lord your God with all your [mind and] heart and with all your being, that you may live.** *(emphasis mine)*

Moses is declaring circumcision as a symbolic act of cutting away the fleshly foreskin of the heart which represents the sinful nature hindering a person to truly love the Lord and live. Jesus said in John 14:15, *"If you [really] love Me, you will keep (obey) My commands."* In other words, you will be a people who obey His voice. God's desire regarding this covenant relationship with His people is a people that are His, loyal and obedient to His voice based on love.

Colossians 2:11-13 speaks of the circumcision of the New Covenant.

In Him also you were circumcised with a circumcision not made with hands, but in a [spiritual] circumcision [performed by] Christ by stripping off the body of the flesh (the whole corrupt, carnal nature with its passions and lusts). [Thus you were circumcised when] you were buried with Him in [your] baptism, in which you were also raised with Him [to a new life] through [your] faith in the working of god [as displayed] when He raise Him up from the dead. And you who were dead in trespasses and in the uncircumcision of your flesh (your sensuality, your sinful carnal nature), [God] brought to life together with [Christ], having [freely] forgiven us all our transgressions.

This scripture draws attention to the direct parallel of being *dead* in trespass and being *brought to life* with Christ by the circumcision of the heart through baptism. If circumcision is a sign of covenant, which represents being spiritually alive and able to love Him fully in loyalty and obedience by faith, then without it one is spiritually dead, unable to walk by faith or remain in allegiance to Him. Therefore, in order to walk with God, His people must bear the token of spiritual circumcision of the heart. This circumcision declares we no longer produce from the loins of the flesh, but rather from the spirit through faith. This is a people who are led by the Spirit and thus as a result walk in victory.

1 John 5:4

> *For whatever is born of God is victorious over the world;*
> *and this is the victory that conquers the world, even our faith.*

Whatever originates from God is born of His Spirit and overcomes the world. For something to be born it must first be conceived. Faith is conceived in the heart, by the spoken word of God, it is not revealed to the natural senses and cannot be incubated in a carnal place (Hebrews 11:1, Romans 10:17, Romans 8). Scripture relates the mind to the production room of God. 1 Peter 1:13 KJV says to gird up the *loins* of our mind. Loins is a metaphorical term that is used to describe fertility and productivity. So Peter was referring to the mind as the production room of the Spirit, where faith is conceived, in our imaginations, the "eyes" of our heart.

When making His promise to Abraham (who was still Abram at the time), regarding the land He would give Him and His posterity, the Lord said in

Genesis 13:14-15

> *Lift up now your eyes, and look from the place where you*
> *are, northward, and southward, and eastward and westward;*
> *For all the land which you see I will give to you and to your*
> *posterity forever.*

The Lord was saying as far as Abraham's "eyes" could see He would give to him. Faith is spiritual vision, the illumination of the eyes of the heart

(Ephesians 1:18-19). With faith, we first must be able to see and understand with the imaginations the will of the Father. It was the loins of a man that bore the natural token of circumcision in the Old Covenant, whereas the spiritual circumcision of the New Covenant after baptism is born in the heart. Paul besought the brethren in Romans 12:2 AMPC to not be conformed or fashioned after the ways of this world but to be transformed by the renewing of the mind, and in this way they would discover the perfect will of God. Because through the circumcision of the New Covenant, the restriction of the fleshly carnal nature has been cut away, believers are now able to discover and obey God's will. In Ephesians 4:23 AMPC, Paul admonishes the Ephesians to be constantly renewed in the spirit of the mind, which displays this renewing as an ongoing process after salvation. Romans 10:17 KJV states that *faith comes by hearing and hearing by the word of God.*

So if the loins of the mind are the production room of faith and faith comes by hearing the word of God, then it is by the Word of God one continues to renew their mind and develop a way of "seeing" that is in line with God's heart and not the world. Romans 12:2 says that to discover the will of God, the mind must be renewed. In other words, if a person is conformed and fashioned after the ways of the world, thinks and lives by the world's standards and morals then that person will not discover the perfect will of God. Why is it important to know the will of God? Because if the will of God is not known, how can one walk in obedience to it? Remember obedience and allegiance is part of covenant. Those who walk according to the ways of the world, which is direct rebellion to His ways, are in covenant with the world and are unable to be led by the Spirit of God. If that is the case, then they are unable to overcome and conquer the world as read in 1 John 5:4.

The one-time act of circumcising the flesh in the Old Covenant was a sign of covenant and a person belonging to God. A similar one-time action of circumcision is introduced in the New Covenant, namely the baptism which signifies faith in Christ's death, burial and resurrection and the stripping of the carnal nature. In the Old Covenant the Israelites repeatedly broke covenant and strayed from walking in His ways even though they bore the token of physical circumcision. The same occurs in the New Covenant, many have departed the faith although they have been baptized (the New Covenant circumcision). So how is it possible for those under the New Covenant to go astray when they are empowered to overcome the flesh? Romans 8 reveals the answer.

In Romans 8, Paul compares the mind of the flesh with the mind of the Spirit. He portrays the mind of the flesh in verse 6 and 7 as sense and reason without the Holy Spirit, death, hostile and not submissive to God. Sense and reason is a mind governed by the flesh, the ways of this world and is what Paul was referring to in Romans 12. Verse 5 of Romans 8 states that those who are according to the flesh, set their minds on things which gratify the flesh. Thus, it is a choice where people set their minds. Those who set their minds on things contrary to God which war against His wisdom (the mind of the Spirit) will gratify the flesh. On the contrary, those who choose to set their minds on His truth and ways in His Word will gratify the Holy Spirit.

The good news is God's people are now empowered by the Holy Spirit to set their minds on things that gratify the Holy Spirit, and to refute arguments, reasonings and every high and vain imagination exalting itself above the knowledge of God by bringing it into the subjection and obedience of the Lord Jesus Christ (2 Corinthians 10:5).

Through this New Covenant circumcision that stripped off the flesh, believers are now able to operate from the mind of the Spirit, which is faith, and to be Spirit-led and please God.

Hebrews 11:6

without faith it is impossible to please Him

Romans 8:8

those who are living the life of the flesh [catering to the appetites and impulses of their carnal nature] cannot please or satisfy God, or be acceptable to Him.

Unbelief Causes People To Stray From Covenant

Hebrews 3:7-12

> *Therefore, as the Holy Spirit says; Today, if you will hear His voice, Do not harden your hearts, as [happened] in the **rebellion** [of Israel] and their provocation and embitterment [of Me] in the day of testing in the wilderness, Where your fathers tried [My patience] and tested [My forbearance] and found I stood their test, and they saw My works for forty years. And so I was provoked (displeased and sorely grieved) with that generation, and said, They always err and are **led astray in their hearts**, and they have not perceived or recognized My ways and become progressively better and more experimentally and intimately acquainted with them. Accordingly, I swore in My wrath and indignation, They shall not enter into My rest. [Therefore beware], brethren, take care, lest there be in any one of you a wicked, **unbelieving heart** [which **refuses to cleave to, trust in, and rely on Him**], leading you to turn away and desert or stand aloof from the living God. (emphasis mine)*

The Holy Spirit is disclosing here that the heart can be hardened through rebellion. What is rebellion? It means to be in direct opposition to authority. For example, God says to do something one way, and we choose to do the opposite. This scripture cautions us to beware of unbelief, because it *develops* in our hearts when we refuse to trust and rely on God. Trust and reliance are core components of faith. Therefore, since faith is the foundation of the New Covenant, a people who have strayed from covenant would be a people walking by sense and reason who have set their minds on the things of this world instead of the Word of God. In a nutshell, people stray from covenant by abandoning their faith. They stop believing God's Word and accept other sources as truth, thus hardening their hearts with unbelief and consequently departing from God.

Evidently we are urged to watch over the condition of our hearts in order to remain in subjection to His authority and ways and not to depart from Him which sadly would disqualify us from possessing the promises and walking in covenant governmental rights. Entering the *rest* refers to the operation of *by His Spirit*, not in the efforts of man or the arm of the flesh, but in the rest of God through faith.

We Cannot Be Led If We Are Dead

Ezekiel confirms that this hard heart of unbelief is what causes one to be *unresponsive* to the leading of the Spirit.

Ezekiel 11:19-20

> *And I will give them one heart [a new heart] and I will put a new spirit within them; and I will take the stony [unnaturally hardened] heart out of their flesh, and will give them a heart of flesh [**sensitive** and **responsive** to the touch of their God], That they may walk in My statutes and keep My ordinances, and do them. And they shall be My people, and I will be their God. (emphasis mine)*

The Amplified Classic Version is brilliant how it expounds on the sentence *give them a heart of flesh*, in brackets saying – *one that is **sensitive** and **responsive** to the touch of their God.*

To be *sensitive* and *responsive* to the touch of God is a person who is led by the Spirit of God. **People cannot be led if they are dead**. They must be alive and awake in order to be sensitive to His leading and promptings. A dead person for example will not react when spoken to or poked. Only something living responds to the touch of someone, which in this case is God. Obviously, in this context it is referring to a spiritual life not physical. Thus, Ezekiel describes unresponsiveness to God's touch as a sign of a hard heart which must be removed in order to restore sensitivity. This is part of the reviving process which involves repentance from unbelief and returning to faith.

Revival – Re-Establishing His People Into Covenant

This is the call of Hosea when He said in chapter 6:1, *Come let us **return** to the Lord*. He is urging His people that unless they return from their unbelieving, backsliding ways which have consequently separated them from God, they will not be able to enter the third day. Romans 8:5 says the mind of the flesh is death, which clarifies why one is in need of reviving. The evident decision of God's people to reject doing things God's way, positions them in a critical, spiritual state of near death, requiring God's intervention to revive them.

Hosea 6:2 says, the Lord, on the third day will "raise up" His people. As discussed in the previous chapter, the Hebrew word for "raise up" translates as: to rise, to establish, to confirm, to fulfil, to be proven, to be made valid, to make stand up. This same Hebrew word for *raise up* is also used throughout scripture in the context of God "establishing" covenant with His people. So if His people need reviving on the second day, it can be deduced that they have departed from covenant, hence the call to *return* in Hosea 6:1.

Consequently, if on the third day His people have been "raised up", it can be ascertained that their covenant with God has been re-established, secured and validated. When God speaks of *establishing* His covenant, He is saying that He is creating a *place* or a *way* for His people to align and be **fixed** in His ways. When they are aligned to His ways they are secure, unshakable and protected. Jesus is the way the Lord made in order to establish His covenant. Jesus is the way back to God, the repairer of the breach, the redemption package to all those lost and gone astray. Scripture teaches that repentance and reconciliation via forgiveness of sin through the blood of Jesus are required for redemption and a return to the Lord. This call to return to the Lord (Hosea 6:1) is declaring the blueprint of the restoration process required to re-establish His church as covenant people.

In New Covenant terms these are people who walk not after the flesh but after the Spirit. Walking in covenant as the Hebrew text indicates, validates, makes firm and causes His people to rise and stand up. This is the position they must take to govern *by His Spirit*. If they walk after the dictates of the flesh, they will not function in His image which is Spirit-led. Thus the New Covenant is the access and way back to operating *in His likeness* and *by His Spirit*.

Chapter 3:

THE REVIVING PROCESS –
THE SPIRIT OF ELIJAH

As discovered in the previous chapter, covenant is the blueprint the Lord set out to reinstate intimacy with His sons and daughters which also restores access to the governmental rights, originally bestowed upon His people at creation. The New Covenant that was prophesied through Jeremiah, Ezekiel, Isaiah and others, promised a picture of eternal hope and a final victory over Satan and his plan for God's creation.

The Spirit Of Elijah – Restoring God's People To The Path Of His Presence

Malachi 3:1 (KJV)

> *Behold, I will send my messenger, and he shall prepare the way before me: and the Lord, whom you seek, shall suddenly come to his temple, even the messenger of the covenant, whom you delight in: behold, he shall come, saith the Lord of hosts.*

This verse is filled with clues and hidden revelation regarding the blueprint of how the Lord restores His people back to walking in His ways. Dissecting this verse in Hebrew offers a clearer understanding.

According to Strong's Concordance the word *messenger* translates as: to dispatch as a deputy; a messenger of God, angel, **prophet, priest or teacher**, ambassador.[19] (emphasis mine)

Strong's Concordance interprets the word *prepare* as: to turn, to face, turn back.[20] The Hebrew meaning of the word *way* according to the Strong's Concordance is: a road, course of life, mode of action, path, custom.[21]

Finally, *"before me"* according to Strong's signifies: the face, countenance, forefront part, presence.[22]

If these defined Hebrew meanings are put together, this is what the prophet Malachi is saying; The messenger operates in the office of a prophet and possesses distinct characteristics as an ambassador, prophet, priest, and teacher. The office of a prophet is one five-fold governmental office that functions in all three of these roles of prophet, priest and teacher. This messenger then, is an ambassador of God who carries a message, via prophesy, intercession or teaching. Malachi describes this prophet as one who will prepare the way of the Lord.

To prepare is to *turn*. Therefore, the message this prophet carries is a message that *turns*. What does it turn? This message turns the hearts of those who hear the message. Where does it turn it to? To the path of the Lord's presence. His presence is His ways, it is where *by His spirit* is discovered, learnt and understood.

---

19   James Strong. Strong's Expanded Exhaustive Concordance of the Bible
        (Nashville: Thomas Nelson, 2009), s.v *"messenger"*
20   Ibid., *"prepare"*
21   Ibid., *"way"*
22   Ibid., *"before me"*

Isaiah 40:3 prophesies this same messenger who shall come to prepare the way before the Lord.

> *A voice of one who cries: Prepare in the wilderness the way of the Lord [clear away the obstacles]; make straight and smooth in the desert a highway for our God!*

The messenger is revealed in Luke 1:15-17 where the angel of the Lord came to Zechariah the high priest prophesying he would father the chosen prophet, John the Baptist.

> *For he will be great and distinguished in the sight of the Lord. And he must drink no wine nor strong drink, and he will be filled with and controlled by the Holy Spirit even in and from his mother's womb. And he **will turn back** and **cause to return many of the sons of Israel to the Lord their God**, And he will [himself] go before Him in the spirit and power of Elijah, to turn back the hearts of the fathers to the children, and the disobedient and incredulous and unpersuadable to the wisdom of the upright [which is the knowledge and holy love of the will of God] – in order to **make ready for the Lord a people [perfectly] prepared [in spirit, adjusted and disposed and placed in the right moral state]**. (emphasis mine)*

Jesus further confirmed John the Baptist as the messenger Malachi was referring to in

Matthew 17:10-13

> *The disciples asked Him, Then why do the scribes say that Elijah must come first? He replied, Elijah does come and will get everything restored and ready. But I tell you that Elijah has come already, and they did not know or recognize him,*

but did to him as they liked. So also the Son of Man is going to be treated and suffer at their hands. Then the disciples understood that He spoke to them about John the Baptist.

This message that turns the people's hearts back to God is an anointing of Elijah that restores and makes ready. What does it make them ready for?

Malachi 3:1 (KJV)

... And the Lord who you seek, shall suddenly come to His temple.

A sudden coming of the Lord. This "sudden" coming of the Holy Spirit to His temple that Malachi was speaking of was fulfilled on the day of Pentecost in Acts 2:1-4.

In Matthew 3:11 (NKJV) John the Baptist is quoted,

I indeed baptize you with water unto repentance: but He who is coming after me is mightier than I, whose sandals I am not worthy to carry. He shall baptize you with the Holy Spirit and fire.

If the *way* of the first coming of Messiah needed to be *prepared,* then how much more the second coming of Messiah? Malachi 4:5 explains that Elijah must come before the great and dreadful day of the Lord. That day mentioned in Malachi 4 is the second coming of the Lord, where He comes to judge the nations of the earth. That is, the "Day of the Lord", the third day, the Day of Ruach.

The Lord's strategy of preparation has not changed. The present-day season is another preparation period where the spirit of Elijah is released to turn hearts back to walking in the path of His presence. This turning of hearts is necessary to step into the third day of governmental power.

The Modern Day Spirit Of Elijah – A Company Of Prophets

Jesus said in Matthew 17:11-12a (AMP)

Elijah is coming and will restore all things; but I say to you that Elijah has come already (emphasis mine)

At first sight, it does not seem to make sense. On one hand Jesus is saying that Elijah is coming (future tense), but on the other hand states that Elijah has already come (past tense). However, Jesus is referring to both events. Firstly, the spirit of Elijah continues to manifest through His prophets preparing the way until the Lord comes (future tense) and secondly, John the Baptist's ministry was a specific instance when the way was prepared for Messiah's manifestation on earth (past tense). Hence Elijah is coming (the continued message of the prophets) and Elijah has come (in the manifestation of John the Baptist at that moment in time). In these last days of preparation (revival), the spirit of Elijah will not just rest upon one person but a company of prophets throughout the earth. Elijah and John the Baptist's ministry were before the outpouring of the Holy Spirit in Acts 2. Therefore, in this day and hour the spirit of Elijah is dispersed upon many via the Holy Spirit, who indeed is the messenger Himself dispensed upon those men and women mantled as the Lord's mouthpieces.

The Messenger Of The Covenant

As previously mentioned, people who have strayed from covenant need reviving. The spirit of Elijah is essentially the spirit of revival and awakening restoring people back into covenant.

Early 2020, I had a very abstract dream that opened up this understanding of the spirit of Elijah being the messenger of the covenant, which restores and revives God's people into covenant. In the dream I saw Elizabeth, John the Baptist's mother, standing on a square platform. That was it, it was a very simple dream. As I woke up, I pondered why the Lord showed me Elizabeth. Was He simply revealing the release of the spirit of Elijah? After a little research, the interpretation I received from the Holy Spirit was that the platform represented "coming to the forefront for all to see". A platform is normally a raised area where something is on display. So the Lord was bringing to the forefront and placing on the platform the mystery of Elizabeth in this hour.

The name Elizabeth is of Hebrew origin and means God's oath, dedicated, consecrated to God.[23] Her name meaning, God's oath, dedicated and consecrated is covenant language. The Lord was showing me that as Elizabeth gave birth to John the Baptist who came in the spirit of Elijah to prepare the way of the Lord, in this very hour the Lord is birthing messengers on the earth, who will carry the message of the covenant that will restore His people into oath, faith, dedication and consecration. This truth is depicted in the second part of Malachi 3:1.

Malachi 3:1b (KJV)

> ..... even the **messenger of the covenant**, whom ye delight in: behold, he shall come, saith the Lord of hosts. (emphasis mine)

The messengers with the spirit of Elijah proclaim the message of the covenant and call God's people back to consecration, faith and holiness.

Note the type of person that the Lord had chosen to prepare the way before Him. It was not a worker of miracles but a *messenger*. A messenger is someone who carries a message. The second part of Malachi 3:1 states that this messenger was a messenger of *covenant*. The message this messenger would carry would be that of restoring God's people back into covenant. Therefore, remembering the study on covenant outlined in chapter 2, this message will

---

23   familyeducation.com, www.familyeducation.com/baby-names/name-meaning/elizabeth, accessed 14 December 2020.

proclaim a return to faith, consecration, intimacy, obedience and allegiance, based on love.

As previously discussed, the Hebrew meaning of Malachi's message of preparation, is one that *turns one back to the path of His presence*. This is the reviving process. In the Lord's presence is where things live, there is no death in His presence. Therefore, in order for His people to be revived and brought back to life, they need to return to the living waters of life, which in scripture is a symbol of His presence. Ezekiel 47:9 says that wherever the river flows everything shall live. The return to the "paths of His presence" and the river of life, is symbolized by John the Baptist's "river of repentance".

The Spirit Of Elijah – The Revival Of Repentance

Mark 1:4 speaks of the type of message John proclaimed.

> *John the Baptist appeared in the wilderness (desert), preaching a baptism [obligating] repentance (a change of one's mind for the better, heartily amending one's ways, with abhorrence of his past sins) in order to obtain forgiveness of and release from sins.*

The message John preached was a message of repentance and remission of sins. This is the message that turns the people's hearts back to the ways of His presence and prepares the *way* of the Lord. John's preaching *is* the message of the covenant which is how the Lord will "revive" His people after the second day, and prepare them to step into the third day.

Chapter 2 unraveled John the Baptist's baptism as the token of the new covenant circumcision of the heart. It was also disclosed that those who strayed from covenant were in rebellion to His way. Luke 1:17 reveals how powerful the message is upon those sent in the spirit and power of Elijah.

Luke 1:17

> *And he will [himself] go before Him in the spirit and power*
> *of Elijah, to turn back the hearts of the fathers to the children,*
> *and the disobedient and incredulous and unpersuadable to*
> *the wisdom of the upright [which is the knowledge and holy*
> *love of the will of God] – in order to make ready for the*
> *Lord a people [perfectly] prepared [in spirit, adjusted and*
> *disposed and placed in the right moral state].*

The Amplified Classic Version beautifully expounds on the transformation of the heart that takes place when the spirit of Elijah moves on a person. This profound anointing to *turn* is demonstrated in even the hardest of hearts, restoring in them a love for the Lord's will and ways. Its targets are the disobedient, incredulous and unpersuadable.

Strong's Concordance translates the word *disobedient* from the Greek as *contumacious* and *unpersuadable*.

The dictionary meaning of *contumacious* is: stubbornly perverse or rebellious, wilfully and obstinately disobedient.[24]

Another word used to describe the heart that the spirit of Elijah would move upon is *incredulous*. Incredulous is defined as: disinclined or indisposed to believe, skeptical, indicating or showing unbelief.[25]

These are all dispositions of the heart disclosed in the previous chapter when discovering how one can walk away from covenant with the Lord. A person possessing an unbelieving, disobedient heart is one who is found dead in sin and unable to be led by the spirit of God, hence their need of reviving that is explained in Hosea 6:2.

---

24   *Dictionary.com,* s.v "contumacious", accessed November 30, 2020,
        https://www.dictionary.com/browse/contumacious
25   *Dictionary.com,* s.v, "incredulous", accessed Nov 30, 2020,
        https://www.dictionary.com/browse/incredulous?s=t

The message of the covenant, repentance and remission of sins, are in fact the reviving process. Being wholeheartedly restored to loving His will and ways is the fruit of repentance that John spoke about in Matthew 3:8. This fruit of repentance bears testimony in lives no longer living according to their own ways, but instead truly submitting to His Lordship. In this hour that is upon us, as the spirit of Elijah is released into the earth, we will see many backsliders come back to the Lord. is a key and powerful scripture to stand upon and declare over prodigals. It doesn't matter how lost or hard-hearted they seem, according to this verse, even the most hardest and unbelieving hearts can be moved and turned by this powerful message and anointing of the spirit of Elijah.

So the question we can ask is why Elijah? Why did John the Baptist come in the spirit and power of Elijah? Why not the spirit and power of Ezekiel, Isaiah, or even Jeremiah? Why does the spirit and power of Elijah prepare the people for the Lord's coming? The keys to unlock these questions can be found when examining the ministry of the ancient prophet Elijah.

Restoration Of The Altar And Foundations Of Government

It is vital to comprehend that we are unpacking a message of the Lord, declaring that the season of ruling and reigning is upon us. To rule and reign are governmental terms and the foundations of governing structures must be sound in order to govern in alignment with heaven's blueprint.

So for the purpose of His people stepping into the third day of ruling and reigning, a reviving process must take place at the end of the second day and part of that process is via the spirit of Elijah. Noteworthily, Elijah was one who restored the altar of the Lord in a time where Israel had erred from the truth and was influenced by Queen Jezebel's idolatrous sorceries and witchcrafts. Part of the restoration of this altar of worship was Elijah's prophetic symbolism of the restoration of government.

1 Kings 18:30-35

> *Then Elijah said to all the people, Come near to me. And all the people came near him. And he repaired the [old] altar of the Lord that had been broken down [by Jezebel]. Then Elijah took twelve stones, according to the number of the tribes of the sons of Jacob, to whom the word of the Lord came, saying, Israel shall be your name. And with the stones Elijah built an altar in the name [and self-revelation] of the Lord. He made a trench about the altar as great as would contain two measures of seed. He put the wood in order and cut the bull in pieces and laid it on the wood and said, fill four jars with water and pour it on the burnt offering and the wood. And he said, do it the second time. And they did it the second time. And he said, Do it the third time. And they did it the third time. The water ran round about the altar, and he filled the trench also with water.*

The altar represents the heart, and in this case, the restoration of the altar represents aligning the heart into its true position in order for the fire to fall on it, confirming an acceptable sacrifice.

The 12 stones represent divine government, restoring the alignment of kingdom government, doing it God's way which is not by might, nor by power, but by His Spirit (Zechariah 4:6).

The sacrifice that Elijah prepared on the restored altar was saturated with water, initiating a move of repentance. This symbolic picture parallels the heart of man being immersed into John the Baptist's river of repentance.

1 Kings 18:37-38

> *Hear me, O Lord, hear me, that this people may know that You, the Lord, are God, **and have turned their hearts back***

[to You]. Then the fire of the Lord fell and consumed the burnt sacrifice and the wood and the stones and the dust, and also licked up the water that was in the trench. (emphasis mine).

In this scripture, the Elijah anointing is seen firsthand as an anointing to *turn* a nation's heart back to the Lord. Hence, the core essence of the spirit of Elijah is an anointing to *turn*. The fire that fell and consumed the sacrifice on Elijah's altar reflects the Acts 2 sudden infilling of Holy Spirit and fire. This confirms John's announcement in Matthew 3:11 of the baptism of fire that would come after his baptism of repentance. The baptism of fire is the empowerment and anointing to accomplish the will of God (Acts 1:8).

Elijah's whole purpose was to reveal the One *true* God, and for the people's hearts to *turn* back to the Lord. The way he proved this was by fire. The fire of God will be the mark upon those who have been awakened by the spirit of Elijah. His fire will descend upon those who have allowed the waters of repentance to wash over their hearts. It will empower them to overcome and its presence on revived people restored into covenant, will reveal to the world the "ONE TRUE GOD". The fire of God will rest upon those set apart and consecrated to the Lord but not upon the lukewarm, indecisive or double-minded people. Those who have been purified by the fire of God will walk in the overcoming fire of God mentioned in Malachi 4:3,

*And you shall tread down the lawless and wicked, for they shall be **ashes under the soles of your feet** in that day that I shall do this, says the Lord of hosts. (emphasis mine)*

The only thing that causes ashes is fire. The reference to ashes under the feet symbolises a people walking in dominion over evil by the fire of God. In the next two chapters we will unpack this concept further. For now let us continue exploring the role of the spirit of Elijah in awakening and reviving the church at the end of the second day.

Preparing The End Time Church To Walk In The Double Portion Mantle

As discussed in chapter 1, the end time church will experience an outpouring of God's spirit in a double portion measure, namely the former and latter rains together. The story of Elijah and Elisha prophesy how the "spirit of Elijah" positions those who have been prepared, to move in a double portion measure of power. 2 Kings 2 relays the events of the last days of Elijah on earth. Elisha, his servant, was determined to remain with his master until he was taken up to heaven. Elijah asked Elisha what he could do for him and Elisha boldly responded with the request of a double portion of Elijah's mantle. Elijah pointed out that this was a "hard" thing, but nonetheless promised him his request if he "saw" Elijah go up with the Lord.

When studying the spirit of Elijah, all elements of scripture noted are relevant from a prophetic perspective. Here a prophetic picture is painted of how the spirit of Elijah prepares the Elisha generation for the coming of the Lord (Elijah's ascent into heaven) and to step into the next season of ruling and reigning. As this end time generation is prepared by the spirit of Elijah, an Elisha generation (the latter day church) will follow, walking in the "former and latter" rains of outpouring power, namely the "double portion". Moreover, as Elijah declared, "this is a hard thing", it will take this latter day generation great focus and resolve to "see" the season of preparation through to the end. In the next chapter we will discuss the refining fire that the spirit of Elijah carries to prepare His people for this task of governing in a double portion mantle of power. Malachi 3:2 asks the question to all in this season of preparation, "Who will endure the day of His coming? For He is a refiner's fire and a fuller's soap." Those who "see through" the process of the refiner's fire will surely enter into the double portion of the latter day, "Third Day Church".

Spirit Of Elijah – Purifying The Mixture

Elijah's ministry, when confronting Queen Jezebel's prophets of Baal, presented a picture of restoration to purity for a people of disillusioned worship. They had forgotten their God and were worshipping around a false altar. Elijah confronted this false idolatry and demonstrated to Israel through power (which happened to manifest as fire), the true God.

Take note here that Elijah's ministry was to *Israel*, God's own people. The messengers who prepare the way of the Lord in the spirit and power of Elijah are ones sent to the Lord's *own people*, His own body, His own church. They are commissioned to confront, challenge and unveil "mixture" that has crept into the worship of the saints, which like the prophets of Baal in 1 Kings 18:26-29 promote a lot of loud noise and ritual, but are void of evident power.

In many ways today, the Body of Christ is in this same position, they have fallen asleep and are in need of reviving. Many have been deceived by the witchcrafts of man-made religion and the mixture of the world which has lured the church to worship around a false altar. This altar takes on the form of social clubs, professionalism, new age philosophies and ideals, self-promotion and a self-serving culture. There is much noise, but no signs and wonders, religious rituals are being practiced, but it is void of the presence of God.

Mixture – The Downfall Of The Kingdom

The story of the tower of Babel is found in Genesis 11. At that time everyone was of one language, accent and mode of expressing.

Verse 4 says,

> *And they said, Come, let us build us a city and a tower whose top reaches into the sky, and let us make a name for ourselves, lest we be scattered over the whole earth.*

The very reason they wanted to build a tower into the sky was to "make a name for themselves". They desired fame, thinking that would secure their kingdom, rather than being scattered abroad.

Verse 5-8

> *And the Lord came down to see the city and the tower which the sons of men had built. And the Lord said, Behold, they are one people and they have all one language; and this is only the beginning of what they will do, and now nothing they have imagined they can do will be impossible for them. Come, let Us go down and there confound (mix up, confuse) their language, that they may not understand one another's speech. So the Lord scattered them abroad from that place upon the face of the whole earth, and they gave up building the city.*

A few significant keys are to be noted here in these verses.

1. The people were unified in their cause. The fact that they were not only speaking the same language but also with the same accent signifies they were one in culture without diversities. There were no diversities in culture. This unity in culture and tongue activated the spiritual law of unity, that they would be able to achieve and succeed in all that they imagined to do. Knowing this spiritual law, the enemy has sought to divide the people of God in culture and cause. Jesus states in Matthew 12:25 that any kingdom that is divided against itself will be brought to desolation and laid waste and no city or house divided against itself will be able to stand. The devil has sought to create division in the kingdom of God by enticing man to build his own kingdoms to make a name for himself. Many have built empires in the "name" of God, but really only seek fame and recognition. These carnal pursuits have disempowered the church of true kingdom authority and have left the church in a carnal immature state. Paul describes a church that

is more interested in identifying itself to man's fame than the fame of Christ as carnal babies still in need of milk. (1 Corinthians 3:1-4)

2. In order for the Lord to interrupt their power, He had to "mix" their language. When something is pure it is powerful, but when it is watered down (mixed), it loses its potency. The mixing of wine is a good example. When wine is watered down, it loses its strength in taste and alcoholic potency. For this reason, the enemy seeks to "mix" the church with unbelief, doubt and worldliness. He knows that if the church of Jesus Christ is spotted and contaminated they are powerless. Hence why the spirit of Elijah is a purifying anointing that will prepare the Bride, presenting her without spot or wrinkle.

The spirit of Elijah causes the hearts of God's people to return to one culture, a kingdom culture of one heart, one mind and one purpose. The pursuit of fame and selfish gain are replaced by a common goal which is to make Jesus famous. In that place victory is assured. In the days of Elijah, the people of God were in confusion. They were mixed with Jezebel's idolatrous worship. Elijah addressed their double-mindedness in 1 Kings 18:21,

> *Elijah came near to all the people and said,* **How long will you halt and limp between two opinions?** *If the Lord is God, follow Him! But if Baal, then follow him. And the people did not answer him a word. (emphasis mine)*

Elijah came to bring the people out of a double-minded state, which in fact is restoring them to faith, the essence of covenant.

James 1:6-8 (KJV)

> *But let him ask in faith, nothing wavering. For he that wavereth is like a wave of the sea driven with the wind and tossed. For let not that man think that he shall receive*

*anything of the Lord. A double minded man is unstable in all
his ways.*

When a person's heart is mixed with doubt and unbelief and not sure of
who God is, it disenables that person to receive from God. The enemy's
purpose is to mix and corrupt the saints' faith so they are ineffective and
unable to reproduce. One of the main spirits that operates under a Jezebelic
influence or government is perversion. The mixture of perversion hinders
power, demonstration and victory.

Matthew 17:14-18

> *And when they approached the multitude, a man came up to
> Him, kneeling before Him and saying, Lord, do pity and have
> mercy on my son, for he has epilepsy (is moonstruck), and he
> suffers terribly; for frequently he falls into the fire and many
> times into the water. And I brought him to Your disciples, and
> they were not able to cure him. And Jesus answered, O you
> unbelieving (warped, wayward, rebellious) and thoroughly
> perverse generation! How long am I to remain with you?
> How long am I to bear with you? Bring him here to Me. And
> Jesus rebuked the demon, and it came out of him, and the boy
> was cured instantly.*

Jesus addressed His disciples quite sternly by stating that they could not
deliver the child of this demon, because of their unbelief and perversion. In
other words, He was insinuating that they had mixture, which was a quite
severe rebuke. However, this scripture portrays how rebellion and unbelief
cause believers to be influenced by a perverse spirit.

The word *perverse* according to the Strong's concordance is: to distort,
corrupt, turn away.[26]

---

26   James Strong. Strong's Expanded Exhaustive Concordance of the Bible
      (Nashville: Thomas Nelson, 2009), s.v *"perverse"*

Thayer's definition of *perverse* is: to oppose, plot against the saving purposes and plans of God, to turn aside from the right path, to pervert, corrupt.[27]

These definitions reveal the enemy's intent to pollute God's people. Perverse people are ones who have been corrupted by mixture (compromise, worldliness, doubt and unbelief) and have turned aside from the right path, ultimately positioning their hearts in opposition to the saving purposes and plans of God! No wonder Jesus was stern in His rebuke to the disciples. The presence of mixture in their lives contaminated their faith and stood in direct opposition to the release of power and authority that was needed to expel this demon.

Spirit Of Elijah Confronts Ahab Leadership And Restores God's People To The Headship Of Father

In the days of Elijah, the mixture of Jezebel's idolatry and perverse Baal worship caused the people to forget who the true God was, and in forgetting who the true God was, they forgot who they were. When believers forget who they are in Christ, they are unable to access their governmental rights of covenant. As a result, they will not demonstrate faith that produces victory and dominion over this earthly realm. This is why Elijah symbolically placed the twelve stones when restoring the altar. The biblical meaning of the number twelve is God's power and authority, and His perfect divine government.[28]

The mixture of a Jezebelic influence seeks to disempower the church by confusing them of their identity. Remember, according to Elijah, the children of Israel were haltering between two opinions. On one hand, the spirit of Elijah challenges God's people to make a choice instead of remaining "on the fence", and on the other hand it reminds the Lord's people of who their father is and who they are as sons and daughters in their covenant relationship with Him.

---

27   Joseph Thayer. Thayer's Greek English Lexicon (Hendrickson Publishers, 1995), s.v *"perverse"*
28   biblestudy.org, www.biblestudy.org/bibleref/meaning-of-numbers-in-bible/12, accessed 27 December 2020.

In order to successfully do this, the Ahab leadership that delivers God's people into this weak polluted state must be confronted.

King Ahab was married to Jezebel, a murderous, covetous harlot, and he allowed her demonic, pagan, wicked idolatry to be practiced in Israel. His passivity and tolerance to this dark evil defiled Israel which brought to the forefront another type of prophet, the prophets of Baal. Baal was the god of rain, lightning and season. Lightning is a prophetic metaphor of the voice of God (Job 37:4 AMPC), so their worship was offering a counterfeit to the true prophetic voice of God. Idolatries around these gods of Baal and Ashteroth, exalted the practices of sexual immorality without restraints, which invited all sorts of vile perversions, child sacrifice, sorcery, witchcraft and mammon worship, just to name a few.

This level of evil raised the need for a prophet who would once again call God's people out of deception of mixture and back into pure consecrated worship. But, Elijah wasn't welcome. He was labelled a troublemaker by the king because Elijah declared famine on the land by reason of their wicked harlotry. Ahab leaders who have tolerated evil and idolatry will accuse true prophets of trouble making, because they bring corrective words that carry consequences and expose their idolatrous leadership.

When Elijah brought the word of the Lord and commanded no rain as a consequence of their idolatry, King Ahab accused him of troubling Israel.

1 Kings 18:17-18

> *When Ahab saw Elijah, Ahab said to him, Are you he who troubles Israel? Elijah replied, I have not troubled Israel, but you have, and your father's house, by forsaking the commandments of the Lord and by following the Baals.*

Elijah, one of many prophets who had not bowed the knee to Baal, was not subject to this kind of manipulation by accusation. Only those who bow the knee and compromise can be manipulated into believing that taking a stand for righteousness is causing trouble. Instead Elijah sprouted back, "It is not I but YOU who has caused this trouble to come upon Israel."

Ahab's weak leadership robbed the Lord's people of understanding their true identity as sons and daughters. They had lost sight of their identity, because they had lost sight of the Father. Ahab leadership reproduces orphans who are motivated by fear.

Romans 8:15,

> *For [the Spirit which] you have now received [is] not a spirit*
> *of slavery to put you once more in bondage to fear, but you*
> *have received the Spirit of adoption [the Spirit producing*
> *sonship] in [the bliss of] which we cry, Abba (Father)!*
> *Father!*

Before people accept Christ they are orphans and their lives are driven by fear. Because of the spirit of adoption, they are no longer slaves to fear, but are yoked to their identity in the Father, and become bold in the face of adversity. A defeated church runs in fear from persecution, but a victorious church is set free from fear, they know who they are and are willing to lay down their lives.

Sons reveal the face of the Father. Christ said to Philip in John 14:9, anyone who has seen Me has seen the Father. The role of the son is to reflect the face of the Father. When the sons of God come forth, they will reflect the face of the Father. The spirit of Elijah will lead God's people back to look into the face of the Father and reflect Him.

Returning The Hearts Of The Father To The Children

Malachi 4 refers to the day of victory, the day of the overcomer. It speaks of the day of the Lord's justice and judgement and the release of the sons of

God. This chapter also teaches that the spirit of Elijah must come before the day of the Lord's power, otherwise there would be destruction.

Malachi 4:5-6 (NKJV)

> *Behold, I will send you Elijah the prophet **before** the coming of **the great and dreadful day of the Lord.** And he will turn the hearts of the fathers to the children, and the hearts of the children to their fathers, lest I come and smite the earth with a curse.*

This addresses people who are not operating under the authority of God, they are walking in lawlessness and are about to implode because of it. A lawless generation arises when Father is taken out of the picture. For this very reason the spirit of Elijah restores the hearts of fathers to the children and the children to the father. When a generation is reunited to Father God they are reconnected to authority and discipline. Without the latter the church is immature, wayward and rebellious. They are indeed dead in works of religion or spotted with the mixture of the world.

The Lord will get His house in order before moving her into victory. Therefore, the spirit of Elijah comes to restore the Lord's house by reinstating governmental fathers and mothers in the church, leading them into the greatest age of earth's history. When genuine fathers are in the seat of government in the church, true apostolic government can function, sound teaching can enable God's people to understand their identity in Christ and responsibilities as sons and daughters, and His people can be trained and instructed in the Word of God instead of worldly, humanistic ideals. When this takes place, the people know their God, stand strong and do mighty exploits (Daniel 11:32b).

The Rise Of The Patriots

You might be asking, "What in the world does the term patriot have to do with the spirit of Elijah? That is a bit random and left field." Well I'm so glad you asked!

In 2019 the word of the Lord came to me regarding an awakening and revival that would take place among His people and this awakening and revival would bring forth a revolution. This word is not only for the body of Christ in the USA, but rather a parallel prophetic analogy of what the Lord is doing throughout the earth in His people.

Unlocking would be the word I would use to describe a ministry trip to the New England area in the USA in October 2019. During a visit to George Whitefield's Church in Newburyport the Lord began to reveal to me a movement that He was arranging in secret which would unearth in the near future and take the world by surprise. This movement is the "Rise of the Patriots", a revolutionary movement that confronts the enemies of this age who seek to steal a generation and future generations.

As is generally known, the "patriots" are those who fought for independence and freedom from the rule of the English crown in the American revolution in the late 1700's. However, there is much more that the Lord is unearthing and wanting us to see regarding this word PATRIOT and the correlation of this term that caused a revolution and birthed a nation into freedom under God.

Origins of the Patriot

Oxford Dictionary describes the word *patriot* as a late 16th century word from Greek *patriotes* or *patrios*, which means "of one's fathers", and from *patris*, meaning "FATHERLAND".[29]

---

[29]   Lexico.com, s.v "*patriot*", accessed October 14, 2019, www.lexico.com/definition/patriot.

Another way of saying "of one's fathers" would be to be called a son, would it not?

A patriot is a son who knows his inheritance and will defend and fight for that heritage until death.

Now interestingly enough, the origin of the term "motherland", derives from the early European settlers in the USA! Two prominent figures of the pilgrim father settlers were John Robinson and William Brewster. While in Holland and planning the emigration to America on the Mayflower, they wrote to Sir Edwyn Sandys in 1617: *"We are well weaned from ye delicate milke of our mother countrie, and enured to ye difficulties of a strange and hard land, which yet in a great parte we have by patience overcome."*[30]

Now the definitions of motherland and fatherland are as follows; Motherland is defined as a country that has or had a lot of colonies while a fatherland is the country of one's birth.[31]

May I say it like this, a fatherland is a place of *origin* which refers to identity. A very interesting key fact during the revolutionary war was the battle cry of the patriot soldiers, "No king, but King Jesus!" In other words, "We are not subjects to a king, but citizens answerable only to God". They were called patriots, because they fought for identity. They were saying our identity is not in the colonies of the motherland, but in our fatherland, our identity is in Christ.

Restoring and Returning to Foundations of Origin and Identity

Isaiah 58:12

And your ancient ruins shall be rebuilt; you shall raise up

---

30 Phrases.org.uk, *s.v.* "motherland", accessed October 14, 2019, www.phrases.org.uk/meanings/mothercountry.html

31 Clay Thompson, "Motherland or Fatherland? It all depends on culture", azcentral.com, February 10, 2015,www.google.com.au/amp/s/amp.azcentral.com/amp/23178367

the foundations of [buildings that have laid waste for] many generations; and you shall be called Repairer of the Breach, Restorer of Streets to Dwell In.

George Whitefield, a founding father of the United states, was a key player in forerunning this awakening of identity in Christ. He was used by God as a mighty instrument to bring forth the First Great Awakening and carried a message of salvation through grace. This message brought division between those who believed salvation through works and those who followed Whitefield's teachings. It was an awakening out of religion and into freedom in Christ.

He was passionate about the separation of Church and State as the State was so corrupt in that day, using religion as a means of political and monetary gain. Even though George Whitefield died years before the Revolutionary War began, he was known as a forerunner and catalyst for the birthing of the United States of America that came from the victory won in that war. He foreran the revolution, opposing the king as head of the church and spiritual matters and passionately preached that God's people should be under the headship of God not a king.

This message imparted identity in a people and encouraged them to pledge allegiance to the crown of King Jesus rather than the crown of the State. The people began to see the Father through the extravagant expression of Christ's love and realized they no longer had to be enslaved to a hypocritical tyranny. They were restored to their fatherland, their place of origin, and were called the patriots.

There is a revival in this message of identity in this present-day. We will see another GREAT AWAKENING in the days to come and surely I believe it is already here. It is a revival where God is releasing men and women of God in this hour who carry and boldly release a message of identity, reminding God's people of who they are before they knew the motherland, before the fall, before the counterfeit covenant. It is returning a people to the fatherland,

Eden, and in that space of restored communion with the Father through the Son Jesus, they will come forth manifesting a selfless boldness and courage to fight and wage war on that which would threaten freedom. This is the rise of the patriots.

Patriotism under Fire – A War on Identity

America has often been judged and slandered by various nations of the earth for its bold and brave patriotism. Even though America's passionate patriotism has been seen as a sense of arrogance and superiority, in these coming days if preserved it will serve as its most powerful weapon against the one world government agenda.

Unfortunately, patriotism is now under fire with the lurking and ever-pressing one world governmental liberal ideas trying to mould a generation with the sole purpose of stealing identity, individualism, national patriotism, and religious liberties. The enemy would seek for America to implode itself by abandoning the patriotism of its foundations and constitution.

I see the Lord causing a revisiting to the foundations upon which the nation of the United States was birthed. There has been a war over the founding constitution with people wanting to move the landmarks and alter the foundation and roots of the nation.

But the Lord is saying in this hour I am once again raising up the patriots which symbolise the anointing of identity, freedom and sonship. And in this hour I am causing those with a message of freedom to arise with the brave heart anointing like that of William Wallace who carry the sound of freedom and identity. They will fearlessly preach identity to a generation where identity is under war, where the scales weigh unjustly in a society that is grossly confused and deceived, bearing an abomination before the Lord. Gender dysphoria, racism, confusion around sexual orientation, denominationalism, are all issues that revolve around identity. These freedom fighters will fearlessly confront those demonic strongholds that pose as spiritual prison guards and set people free of the shackles that bind them in this demonic deception.

The Sound Of A Second Revolution – The Sons Are Coming

There is a battle against the truth of the covenant of freedom through Christ with a counterfeit expression of freedom that is guising itself under the banner of a false Christ, sprouting and declaring Jezebelic heresies.

Just like in the days of Elijah, there is a remnant in the body who have not bowed their knee to the sorceries and idolatries of Jezebel. There is a company of patriots arising, mantled in the spirit and power of Elijah, restoring many back to the fatherland. Those being reconciled back to Father will be restored into covenant sonship and will possess a fearless boldness against the deceptions that held them prisoner. They will be mantled with the anointing of Jehu and will uproot the demonic mixture of Jezebel from their midst.

A fearless few like Gideon's army are rising, ones who don't want to play church, but actually are sold out to the cause of freedom, again revisiting foundations. The sound of the message of identity that was deposited into the New England soil by George Whitefield is surfacing. This sound of freedom is vibrating from the ground and I personally engaged with this sound as I stood on this very soil.

The sound of a revolution is being birthed by a message of awakening to identity. The sons are arising, and the reflection of the face of Jesus they carry will not be what the religious recognise as Jesus. They are looking for Him to come in a different way, preconceived in their own minds.

But the sons are coming, they are awakening to who they are and the power that will be released through this knowledge will cause a revolution. A revolt is erupting against the principalities and rulers of darkness, that deceive and whisper lies to people regarding their identity.

Yes, it's a time to call to arms and awaken those who are asleep in religion and confusion. It's time for a sound to cut through the airways that is unlike any other sound and shock and shake awake a people back into reality from their fantasy land stupor. This generation must realise it is in dire straits and in desperate need of a thunderous move of God's hand that will cause them to know Him.

The American revolution is a prophetic picture of what I believe the Lord is prophesying in this time: as one nation was born under God, so there is one body of Christ coming forth as sons finding their battle cry "No other king than King Jesus!" It will be a bride who is FULLY AWAKE, FULLY IN LOVE and totally divorced from any allegiance to the motherland, the devil and his counterfeits. They are the patriots fighting a war on mixture and perversion that is rooted in the lack of identity.

A revolution will, therefore, rise against the tyranny of the demonic principalities lying and deceiving a generation to death and hell. Sons understanding who they are will be the ignition point of this revolt against such demonic darkness of this hour and the light of the knowledge of the sons will pierce the darkness.

Here come the sons, this is the rise of the patriots.

In these last hours or even moments of the second day, the Lord is indeed releasing the spirit of Elijah throughout the earth to revive the church. God is heralding through His messengers of covenant a call to return to the paths of His presence. This present-day the Lord is pouring water over the altar of the hearts of His people via His messengers who carry the message of repentance. Through these messengers the Lord is calling His people back to the one true God and away from the mixture of the world, self-exalting worship and idolatrous witchcraft. He is calling His beloved back into covenant, to walk by faith, to become awakened, revived, and restored into sonship. In other words, a people prepared and made ready for the Lord.

Chapter 4:

PROMOTION COMES AFTER THE FIRE

Spirit-filled believers tend to mainly relate the fire of God to the day of Pentecost when the Holy Spirit descended in tongues (Acts 2). Signs, wonders, miracles, salvations, mighty displays of power are what many expect regarding the manifestations of the fire of God. Yes this is true, but do not forget the refining, purifying fire, which a lot of Christians shy away from. This purifying fire, as described in Malachi 3:3, brings forth the overcomer walking in the fire of God (Malachi 4), in the "Day of the Lord".

Malachi 3 verse 1 foretold the messenger who would come in the spirit of Elijah and prepare God's people for the Messiah in whom they *sought*. They were seeking God fervently for the promise of Messiah to manifest.

Now let's continue this narrative in Malachi 3:2 (KJV),

> *But who may **abide** the day of His coming? And who shall **stand** when He appeareth? For He is like a refiner's fire and a fullers' soap. (emphasis mine)*

Another translation of the word "abide" is "endure". Why would those questions need to be asked? The word endure would not normally be a word I would think of when positioning my heart in seeking the Lord for encounter. Endure Him? What could this mean? Thankfully the latter part of the verse provides more clarification. It describes the day of His coming marked by His refining, purifying fire. Using the word endure would suggest a temptation to run away from or even reject His refining fire. Why would that be?

According to the Strong's concordance, *abide/endure* in the Hebrew translates as: to keep in (to measure - comprehend - discern), to maintain, to nourish, sustain, receive, make provision, support, endure.[32]

In other words, questions asked here are these; "Who will make provisions for this refiner's fire?", "Who will make room for it?", "Who will receive it?", "Who will nourish and feed it?", "Who will remain in it?", "Who will properly measure and discern what the day of His coming is?"

Or on the contrary, "Who will shut it out?", "Who will run from it?", "Who will not discern it, but criticize it?", "Who will blame the devil or people for it?", "Who will say this message is not from God, because it's too forthright and challenging?"

Strong's Concordance translates the word *stand* as: to remain, take one's stand, tarry, delay, remain.[33]

Will we embrace the day of His coming and stand when He appears or run for the hills?

---

32   James Strong, Strong's Expanded Exhaustive Concordance of the Bible
        (Nashville: Thomas Nelson, 2009), s.v. *"abide"*
33   Ibid., *"stand"*

Is The Lord's Coming Unicorns, Rainbows And Lollipops?

The Lord, through the prophet Malachi, is not asking if we will endure because He's going to show up with butter cakes, unicorns, rainbows and lollipops. However, the verbs to endure or to stand register the connotation of a challenge that could tempt one to run away. This shows that the Lord is coming in a way that might be uncomfortable for the flesh. In fact, 2 Timothy 4:3 explains that there will be a time where people will not want to *endure* sound doctrine;

> *For the time is coming when [people] will not tolerate (endure) sound and wholesome instruction but, having ears itching [for something pleasing and gratifying], they will gather to themselves one teacher after another to a considerable number, chosen to satisfy their own liking and to foster the error they hold.*

In other words, people want to hear what makes them "feel" good and that which doesn't challenge or bring them out of denial with the error they hold. Sometimes to hear what we need to hear isn't comfortable for the flesh. However, we need to be reminded that in Galatians 6:8, Paul instructs us that if we sow to the flesh we will reap corruption.

Strong's concordance interprets the word *corruption* in the Greek as; decay and ruin.[34]

This clearly is not what we or the Lord desire for our lives. So receiving the Lord in the way in which He desires to come to us, is sowing to our spirit and the second part of Galatians 6:8 says that if we sow to the spirit we will reap everlasting life.

---

34   James Strong, Strong's Expanded Exhaustive Concordance of the Bible (Nashville: Thomas Nelson, 2009), s.v. *"corruption"*

The Purification Process

Malachi 3:3

> *He will sit as a **refiner and purifier of silver**, and He will purify the priests, the sons of Levi, and **refine** them like **gold and silver**, that they may offer to the Lord **offerings in righteousness**. (emphasis mine)*

This verse reveals the way He will appear to His people; namely like a refiner's fire and a fullers soap. Remember verse 1 in Malachi 3 says, *the Lord whom you seek, He will come.* When people seek the Lord with all their hearts, they begin to draw near to God.

James 4:8 (NKJV)

> *Draw near to God and He will draw near to you. Cleanse your hands, you sinners; and purify your hearts, you double-minded.*

If you are seeking Him, He will come, but He will come to purify. Hebrews 12:29 says that our Lord is indeed a consuming fire. If you pursue the Lord, you will meet with His fire. The closer you get to Him, the more fire you will experience and the more you will be purified. What will we be purified from? James 4:8 exhorts the believer to be purified from double-mindedness in the heart, along with cleansing the hands (which symbolise works – or what you put your hand to). In the Amplified Classic Version this verse suggests the heart is purified from disloyalty to God and spiritual adultery.

The second part of Malachi 3:3 says, *He will purify the priests and the sons of Levi.* So how does that relate to us now? Through the finished work of the cross, we have been promoted from slaves to kings and priests. That office of a priest is no longer solely assigned to the descendants of Levi, but we too now inherit this position through the blood of Christ who is from the order of Melchizedek (Hebrews 7, Revelation 1:6).

Kings and priests are governmental positions. Through Jesus' work at Calvary we have been promoted to rule and reign with Him.

Hence in the new covenant the Lord will deal with His people as He dealt with His priests. He will refine them like gold and silver, so they may offer offerings of righteousness.

Proverbs 17:3 (The Passion Translation)

> *In the same way that gold and silver are refined by fire, the*
> *Lord purifies your heart by the tests and trials of life.*

Notice in Proverbs 17:3, that the Lord likens our hearts to silver and gold. He causes our hearts to go through a refining process, consisting of tests and trials of life. Jesus said we would endure trials and tribulations, but to be of good cheer for He has overcome them (John 16:33). The Lord doesn't bring the trial, He does not inflict or afflict us with sickness, tragedies and traumas to test us. However, in an imperfect world hardships and difficulties are inevitable. Jesus encourages us that as He has overcome, so can we through Him. The Lord does not create the drama or hardship. Trials occur at times beyond our control, or because of certain decisions or choices we have made. Nonetheless, whether it was caused by the devil or man, the Lord will turn it for our good. (Genesis 50:20, Romans 8:28)

Rarely are silver and gold found in a pure state. They are usually mixed with other substances. In order for these precious metals to gain value, they must be separated from other substances, which is accomplished through a firing method. The fire melts the precious metal, thereby bringing its impurities, also known as dross, to the surface. Once the impurities are removed, the silver and gold appear more brilliant and clean. Thus, our hearts undergo a refining process, we can expect dross to arise, enabling the Lord to discard it and deliver our souls from that which would hinder us from walking in full freedom of our glorious inheritance in Christ Jesus.

The Impurities Of Dross

In Ezekiel 22:18 (New American Standard Bible) the Lord refers to the *rebellious* house of Israel as dross.

> *Son of man, the house of Israel has become dross to Me; all of them are bronze and tin and iron and lead in the furnace; they are the dross of silver.*

Jeremiah 6:28-30 (NASB) also addresses the rebellious house of Israel and explains that the refining of their trials and judgements continued in vain, not separating the dross from Israel. Consequently, the Lord rejected them.

> *All of them are stubbornly rebellious, Going about as a talebearer. They are bronze and iron; they, all of them are corrupt. The bellows blow fiercely, the lead is consumed by the fire; In vain the refining goes on, But the wicked are not separated. They call them rejected silver, Because the Lord has rejected them.*

WOW! The Lord here is metaphorically relating the sins and impurities in Israel, such as talebearing, corruption and rebellion to inferior metals that need to be purified. Israel was the Lord's piece of silver, His redemptive picture of salvation coming to the nations. However, in Jeremiah's time, they yoked themselves with contamination and refused to be purged of their wickedness. The Lord, therefore, turned His back on them and they were taken into Babylonian captivity.

Isaiah 1:21-23 (NASB) also refers to the sins of the house of Israel as dross.

> *How the faithful city has become an harlot, She who was full of justice! Righteousness once lodged in her, but now murderers. Your silver has become dross, Your drink diluted with water. Your rulers are rebels and companions of thieves; Everyone loves a bribe and chases after rewards. They do not defend the orphan, Nor does the widow's plea come before them.*

Proverbs 25:4 (NASB)

> *Take away the dross from the silver, And there comes out a vessel for the smith;*

These above mentioned verses relate dross to sin with rebellion (in opposition to God's authority and kingship) as the common theme. The prophet Samuel likened rebellion to witchcraft (1 Sam 15:23). Galatians 5:19-21 lists witchcraft as a work of the flesh. In other words, those things that work in and by the flesh in opposition to God. The refiner's fire, therefore, needs to come upon the heart and separate attitudes or belief systems that are operating in rebellion to the truth of God.

According to Strong's concordance, the word *refine/purge* in the Hebrew translates as: clarify, distil, strain.[35]

To clarify means to remove mixture or to distinguish. When a Christian is mixed they aren't distinguished from the world. They don't stand out or appear any different. As mixed believers we are ineffective in our ability to walk in our inheritance and bring kingdom on earth. In chapter 3 we visited this truth regarding mixture and weakening power.

---

35   James Strong, *Strong's Expanded Exhaustive Concordance of the Bible* (Nashville: Thomas Nelson, 2009), s.v. "*refine*"

To *purge* in the Oxford dictionary signifies: to rid (someone or something) of an unwanted quality, condition, or feeling.[36]

Strong's concordance explains the word *purify* in the Hebrew as: to be bright, to be pure, unadulterated (not mixed with another), innocent or holy (separate), to make clean.[37]

Spiritual adultery is when our worship, adoration, faith and obedience are placed elsewhere apart from God. It doesn't always look like obvious "sins". Fear is one impurity in the heart that if yielded to, will cause us to abandon our belief and make decisions outside of faith. When spiritual adultery takes place, we are mixed, dull, lacking brightness, dirty and contaminated. According to the Hebrew meaning of *purify*, the purpose of the refiner's fire is to cleanse and separate us from contamination, thereby causing us to shine brightly. This enables us to now stand out distinguished from the world as holy and consecrated unto the Lord, reflecting His light and glory.

Sometimes in our Christian life, we can be unaware of things hidden in our hearts that hinder us from walking in the full freedom of our inheritance bought with Jesus' blood. Romans 1:17 states *the just shall walk by faith*. Faith is how we govern with Christ and also how we received our salvation through grace. Therefore, we continue to walk out our salvation and freedom by faith.

The Lord refines us as gold and silver by separating or bringing to the surface in our hearts things that would contaminate pure faith and hinder us from becoming more than overcomers.

The fire separates the unwanted mixture of unbelief, rebellion, idolatry, stubbornness, pride, fear and hurts that lie in the heart. He knows what is in our hearts, even when we are completely unaware. He knows our blind spots

---

36   *Lexico.com*, s.v "purge", accessed July 19, 2021,www.lexico.com/definition/purge.
37   James Strong, Strong's Expanded Exhaustive Concordance of the Bible
       (Nashville: Thomas Nelson, 2009), s.v. *"purify"*

and areas of denial that cause us to repeatedly stumble, hindering us from successfully achieving and accomplishing our heavenly assignments. These blind spots include, pride (striving, self-reliance, overexaggerated opinions of ourselves, self-preservation and performance mindsets), competition, jealousy, stubbornness, selfishness, insecurities (orphan-related belief systems), wrong belief systems contrary to the Word of God (unbelief and new age philosophies), fear (of man, failure, abandonment, solitude, rejection, the future), hurts and unforgiveness etc. The refiner's fire brings the dross and impurities in our lives to the surface for the purpose of repenting and receiving healing and wholeness.

The Lord, like the silver and goldsmith, will deal with his people in order for them to display the quality and character of what silver and gold represent. If we understand this process, we are more likely to yield to it, knowing it is the hand of the Lord and not some foreign attack from the enemy or something to be afraid of.

Silver

Silver symbolises the redemptive work of Christ. The refining process of silver in our lives brings forth the redemption of the finished work of the cross.

To redeem is to regain possession in exchange for payment. Jesus is our redeemer who bought our freedom, deliverance and salvation with His precious blood.

Our enemies are His and the Lord promises to deal with His enemies by fire. Psalm 97:3 (NKJV) says;

> *A fire goes before Him, and burns up His enemies round about.*

Enemies of the soul are purified in the refining process of silver. The Lord in His mercy and lovingkindness will purge and purify the areas where the enemy has left a mark and created demonic strongholds in our soul.

At times when the Lord exposes our impurities, it can appear as if we are reliving these things. We could feel awful about ourselves or experience wounding or pain in the heart with the same intensity as when it initially happened. However, it is just heat of the refining fire bringing the "dross" to the surface, so the silver or goldsmith (the Lord) can remove it. In other words, the impurity is brought to our attention, so we can see it clearly for what it is and repent, therefore, disallowing its rights to remain within our hearts and denying the enemy's access to legally possess territory in our lives.

Repentance is the act that releases the redemptive power of the blood to cleanse and rid us of the impurities and bring healing and wholeness.

How Is The Refining Fire Activated In Our Life?

His Word

Jeremiah 23:29

> *Is not my word like fire [that consumes all that cannot endure the test?] says the Lord, and like a hammer that breaks in pieces the rock [of most stubborn resistance]?*

The Word of God carries the fire of purging and purifying. When we receive a prophetic rhema Word of God through a prophesy or the written Word, the Lord can use it to destroy the enemies of our soul that hinder us from enduring. His Word that is like a fire challenges the heart and exposes stubborn resistance within us that prevents us from walking in victory.

The Fire of His Presence

Psalm 97:5

> *The hills melted like wax at the presence of the Lord, at the presence of the Lord of the whole earth.*

To melt wax you need a flame. So, if the hills are melting like wax then this would suggest that the presence of the Lord is a flame of fire. As we have already noted, the Lord Himself is fire (Hebrews 12:29), therefore drawing near and being in His presence is drawing near to His fire. Pursuing intimacy with the Lord will bring about a purification process in one's life.

The Fire of His Love

Song of Solomon 1:2 KJV

> *Let him kiss me with the kisses of his mouth: for thy love is better than wine*

According to Strong's Concordance, *kiss* in the Hebrew is *nashaq*; it is a primitive root with the notion "*to fasten upon*".[38]

This word is identical to the Hebrew word *nawsak*; which means to *catch fire/to kindle*.[39]

These words have a close correlation to the Hebrew word *chazaq,* which also implies to fasten upon, to *conquer or seize*. This word *chazaq,* is the same Hebrew word used for "show Himself strong" in 2 Chronicles 16:9. *Chazaq* is also related: to *chashaq* which signifies to: *delight in, to love, to join, to desire, but also to **deliver**.*[40]

---

38   James Strong, Strong's Expanded Exhaustive Concordance of the Bible
       (Nashville: Thomas Nelson, 2009), s.v. "*kiss*"
39   Ibid., "*burn, kindle*"
40   Ibid., Strong's number 2388, 2836

I wondered why the Shulamite woman in Song of Solomon first says, *"Let"* Him kiss me with the kisses of his mouth. It wasn't until I read the Hebrew meaning of the word kiss, that I began to understand this language. She is speaking to her heart, "Heart surrender to these kisses, *let* Him kiss me, desire these kisses of His mouth for His love is better than wine."

Wine is symbolic of the world's counterfeit intoxication that His beloved runs to for comfort, joy, peace, fulfilment, love etc. The world can provide all these temporary benefits for a moment, but it leaves you empty in the end. We seek gratification by chasing mammon, relationships and success in order to find peace, joy and love. However, it is a temporary satisfaction which leaves you with a heart "hangover" from grief and internal despair.

So as the Shulamite discovered, in order to receive His kiss of love, which is His fire, surrender is the key. In light of the Hebrew meanings of the words explained in Song of Solomon 1:2, this is my interpretation of the Shulamite's prayer in her deep pursuit of her beloved,

> *"There is nothing like Your love. "Kiss" me with the fire of Your love, deliver and conquer my heart by Your deep desire for me, a love as strong as death. Show Yourself strong and avenge the enemies of my soul that have kept us apart and hindered our intimacy. I yield to the kisses of Your fire. Lord, I say come and seize my heart as Yours and Yours alone! For I know this world has nothing to offer me, it is empty and futile and doesn't come close to Your love."*

His fire is His response to a lover who seeks Him. His fire delivers His beloved from whatever may seek to keep her spotted and hold her heart captive from fully loving Him. He burns up those enemies of intimacy within her heart and urgently calls her to cut loose (through repentance) of all attachments to worldly things and accompanying ideologies.

The fire of God separates, purifies, sanctifies and causes us to be spotless from the world.

When kissed by the fire of His love, it will bring a separation and sanctification. It will purify the spots that have been left by the world. He is marking His beloved with the fire of His love, to truly stand out as a beacon of truth to the world.

He is our kinsman redeemer, the refiner of silver bringing forth His redeemed people as His prized possession and a doorway of redemption for the nations.

Gold

Not only are we purified in the fire of God, we are also forged and fortified, which means to create something strong, enduring and successful. This process happens in the purifying of gold. Gold symbolises the nature and character of God, the mature sons reflecting the Father. This is when we begin to step into possession, and governmental authority and power.

2 Timothy 2:12 (NKJV)

> *If we **endure**, we shall also **reign** with Him; If we deny Him,*
> *He also will deny us. (emphasis mine)*

This verse unfolds endurance as the prerequisite to reigning with Him. Endurance is the fortitude developed in the furnace of affliction that enables us to walk in our governmental capacity.

Isaiah 48:10-11

> *Behold I have refined you, but not as silver; I have tried and*
> *chosen you in the furnace of affliction. For my name sake,*

for My own sake, I do it [I refrain and do not utterly destroy you]; for why should I permit My name to be polluted and profaned [which it would be if the Lord completely destroyed His chosen people]? And I will not give My glory to another [by permitting the worshipers of idols to triumph over you].

Isaiah 48 reminds us to bear the name of the Lord and walk in His glory. He doesn't refine us as silver (bringing forth redemptive freedom and purity in our lives), but in the furnace of affliction, which is the purification process of gold. The testing of our faith through affliction prepares us to carry governmental authority and power. The Lord will not share His glory with another, therefore we are called, as ambassadors of Christ, to bear His name throughout the nations. He purifies us in the furnace of affliction because we carry His name. The Lord says He doesn't want His name to be profaned. For this reason, He cannot give us too much too soon, because we will blow up and hurt others. For instance, when people step into governmental positions or are given kingdom responsibilities prematurely without being tested in the fire, they will degrade the name of the Lord and display a negative representation of Christianity, by falling into sin and wounding others or giving into the enemy's pressure to quit. Thus, if you are not fortified in the fire, you will surrender to the enemy in defeat as he triumphs over you.

The Lord once spoke to me and said, "Anita, if you can endure My fire which is hotter than any fire, then the fires of the enemy will never overcome you."

Trials, tribulations and persecutions refine us like gold. This process is where our faith is tested, which produces character to possess the promises.

1 Peter 1:6-7

*[You should] be exceedingly glad on this account, though now for a little while you may be distressed by trials and suffer temptations, So that [**the genuineness**] of your faith*

*may be tested, [**your faith**] **which is infinitely more precious***
than the perishable gold which is tested and purified by fire.
[This proving of your faith is intended] to redound to [your]
praise and glory and honour when Jesus Christ the Messiah
and anointed one is revealed. (emphasis mine)

What are the temptations? These include quitting, going our own way and escaping pressing situations and trials by our own efforts instead of using faith. Trials purify that which is not genuine in our faith and will not stand up under the test.

However, that which is genuine also needs to be tested. Is it faith or a good idea? If it is God, it will endure the test. Furthermore, our trust in God will be tested in this test of faith. If it is God, do we trust Him in the process? If it is not genuine, it needs to be exposed and purified.

Genuine means to be sincere without ulterior motives or self-serving agendas. We can receive an instruction from God, but our core motive in achieving or accomplishing it must be examined. When something is fake it fails. Therefore, our motives and our faith need to go through the fire to be tested.

The testing of our faith separates us from the cares of the world and our reliance upon it.

Romans 5:3-4

Moreover [let us be full of joy now!] let us exult and triumph
in our troubles and rejoice in our sufferings, knowing that
pressure *and **affliction** and **hardship** produce patient and*
unswerving endurance. And endurance (fortitude) develops
maturity of character (approved faith and tried integrity).
*And character of this sort produces joyful and **confident***
hope of eternal salvation. *(emphasis mine)*

Trials and tribulations refine us to the point where we are set free from cares, distractions and worldly pursuits. We become heavenly focused and kingdom motivated instead of self-driven and earthly-minded.

Romans 5:4 describes endurance as the attribute that develops maturity of character, which is approved faith and tried integrity or faith and faithfulness. The latter traits produce joyful and confident hope of eternal salvation. I always wondered what this verse meant and would think to myself, "I know I have eternal salvation, God, but how is this trial bringing that forth? Does it mean You are taking me through trials so it will produce a joy in me to die and an expectation to leave this earth?" What it means is this, the trial that has produced endurance, leads us to maturity where we are separate from the world and no longer dictated to by the earthly realm. Our joy doesn't come from our earthly pursuits but from our eternal inheritance. This according to Paul is maturity of character. Paul consistently reminds us throughout his epistles that carnality is spiritual immaturity. To be moved by the occurrences in the natural realm shows we are still earthly minded and therefore spiritually immature. However, when we are free of these cares and concerns, we can truly be led by the Spirit of God, which is the mark of the sons of God who will govern in third day resurrection power.

Perfection Is Not The Goal But Rather Maturity

One day I was sitting with the Lord and I must have positioned my heart in a striving way within my internal meditations. I was worried about a lot of problems and concerns that needed to be aligned, fixed, solved and answered. The Lord so graciously interrupted my heart ponderings and whispered to me, *"Anita perfection is not the goal, but purity."* When the Lord speaks, the simple understanding follows His soothing, calming voice. I realised I was striving for everything to be perfect, but the Lord was seeking purity. The aim of His refining process is to bring about purity. Purity is in relation to heart motive rather than ability in skill or successful achievements. In addition, everyone's walk is dissimilar, making the refining process and the areas of dealing with us in different season, relative to our callings. The Lord will cause us to overcome and He desires to burn out of our lives the enemies associated with hindering the fulfilment of our heavenly assignments. My areas of forging and refining may be different from yours. Hence we aren't to look around comparing each other's imperfections, but rather grasp how detrimental these exposed impurities are for our walk. The higher the level of promotion and rank in the kingdom, the more intense the firing will be. The Lord will often take you through another firing before each promotion.

James tells us in the verse below that we need endurance, steadfastness and patience (produced through trials and tribulations) in order to be fully developed, lacking nothing. However, it is not referring to perfection in the common context of the word, but instead completeness and maturity, the required qualities for ruling and reigning with Christ.

James 1:2-4

> *Consider it wholly joyful, my brethren, whenever you are enveloped in or encounter trials of any sort or fall into various temptations. Be assured and understand that the trial and proving of your faith bring out **endurance and steadfastness and patience**. But let endurance and steadfastness and patience have full play and do a thorough work, so that you may be [people] perfectly and fully developed [with no defects], lacking in nothing. (emphasis mine)*

According to the Oxford dictionary, *persistence* is doing something despite difficulty or delay in achieving success.[41]

Endurance is the ability to endure an unpleasant or difficult process or situation without giving way.[42]

---

41   *Lexico.com, s.v. persistence,* accessed 5/8/21, www.lexico.com/definition/persistence
42   Ibid., *endurance*

Patience is the capacity to accept or tolerate delay, problems or suffering without becoming annoyed or anxious.[43]

Trials can include delay, suffering, unpleasant and difficult processes, unjust situations and hardships. These produce in us the abilities to stand and not quit (endurance), remain peaceful and trusting, without losing the plot (patience), and continue in obedience despite the outcome not happening in our timing or not gaining our desired result (persistence). These qualities reveal and produce a proved faith and tried integrity in our lives where the Lord can trust us with much.

When I was pregnant I battled impatience in the last stages of pregnancy, I was uncomfortable, I couldn't sleep properly, I felt heavy, over it etc. I would walk as much as possible to bring on labour.

We can often try in our own strength to bring on the birthing process of things we have been carrying in faith. In the last season of pregnancy you feel completely confined and have had enough, consequently attempting to give birth prematurely.

But we need to let patience have its perfect work so we are fully developed, lacking in nothing. During the season of confinement the promise is hidden as it is being formed and patience is working to bring that promise to fulfilment so it will not be lacking in anything. Think about it, if a baby is born prematurely it can suffer many complications due to immature physical development. These can include sight, hearing, breathing just to name a few. The questions posed to us then are the following. Are we going to do things in our own strength? Are we going to run before our time? Do we give God conditions regarding the timing of His promises being fulfilled? The waiting can prove to be a fiery trial and testing of our faith, but it is so we reach maturity with our faith and promise fully developed, lacking in nothing.

---

43   Ibid., *patience*

James 1:12

> *Blessed is the man that is patient under trial and stands up*
> *under temptation, for when he has stood the test and been*
> *approved, he will receive [the victor's] crown of life which*
> *God has promised to those who love Him.*

Patience here in the Greek signifies the same as in Romans 5:3, namely to remain and persevere, and to have fortitude.[44] Fortitude means to have courage in pain or adversity.

Hebrews 10:36

> *For you have need of steadfast patience and endurance, so*
> *that you may perform and fully accomplish the will of God,*
> *and thus receive and carry away [and enjoy to the full] what*
> *is promised.*

In order to perform the will of God, and receive God's promises, patience and endurance (perseverance) are needed! Thus, remaining obedient is not a single act, but it requires faithfulness to God's instruction for however long the season lasts.

Promotion Comes After The Fire

Esther went through a process of purification before her promotion into her governmental position of ruling and reigning.

The example of Esther is a prophetic example of the preparation of the bride.

---

44   James Strong, Strong's Expanded Exhaustive Concordance of the Bible
         (Nashville: Thomas Nelson, 2009), s.v. *"patience"*.

I believe this is the refining process of how the Lord deals with His sons and daughters, kings and priests ordained to rule and govern with Him on earth as it is in heaven.

Esther's first process was *purification*. For six months she was rubbed with the oil of myrrh (Esther 2:12).

In biblical times, myrrh was used as one of the ingredients in the anointing oil and also as a perfume. This anointing oil was to sanctify and separate the temple, the utensils and the priests as holy unto the Lord (Exodus 30:22-30). It was also used to embalm and purify the dead for burial.

This purification process is symbolic of the Lord's refining fire preparing His beloved to rule in a governmental position.

Another example of the fire preceding promotion into governmental authority was Shadrach, Meshach and Abed-Nego (Daniel 3).

They were governors, so they already held positions of authority in the land of Babylon and served under an ungodly king. Then the testing of their faith came which was a furnace of affliction or in simple terms persecution. However, they did not deny their faith and were promoted to another level of government (Daniel 3:30).

What Is An Offering Of Righteousness?

Now that we understand the purifying of gold and silver, let us take a look at the second part of Malachi 3:3.

> *He will sit as a refiner's fire and a purifier of silver, and He will purify the priests, the sons of Levi, and refine them like gold and silver,* ***that they may offer to the Lord offerings in righteousness.*** *(emphasis mine)*

The Lord is highlighting the necessity of offering sacrifices in purity in order for them to be received by Him.

In the old covenant there were certain rules the priests had to follow in order to offer sacrifices correctly unto the Lord. For instance, regarding various sacrifices, they had to offer animals without spot or blemish (Leviticus 1:3, 22:19). Unfortunately, according to Malachi 1:8, the priests did not obey God's instructions with their sacrifices. But how does this relate to us today?

Let us go to the first mention of a sacrifice, namely in the story of Cain and Abel. Abel's sacrificial offering was acceptable to God, whereas Cain's was rejected (Genesis 4:3-7). Why was Cain's offering rejected?

The answer is found in Genesis 4:6-7

> *And the Lord said to Cain, Why are you angry? And why do you look sad and depressed and dejected? If you **do well**, will you not be accepted? And if you do not do well, sin crouches at your door, its desire is for you, but you must master it. (emphasis mine)*

Abel offered what God required. So it was obedience that displayed an act of faith, which is pleasing to God (Hebrews 11:6). Cain, on the other hand, did not offer according to what God had asked. The Lord then said, "If you do well you will also be accepted."

The Brown-Driver-Briggs Hebrew dictionary defines "do well" as: to be *pleasing, to do right.*[45]

To be pleasing to God is to walk by faith, in obedience and trust, to do things *God's way*. But in essence, Cain's offering displayed an independent, rebellious heart saying, "I will do this walk with you God on my terms".

---

45   Enhanced Brown-Driver-Briggs Hebrew and English Lexicon, Clarendon Press, 1977 *"do well"*

Understanding a New Covenant Sacrifice

Romans 12:1 speaks of a new covenant sacrifice that is acceptable to the Lord.

> *I appeal to you therefore, brethren, and beg of you in view of [all] the mercies of God, to make a decisive dedication of your bodies [presenting all your members and faculties] as a living sacrifice, holy (devoted, consecrated) and well pleasing to God, which is your reasonable (rational, intelligent) service and spiritual worship.*

Interestingly, though Jesus fulfilled the law (He is the ultimate sacrifice for our sins) and abolished the requirements of approaching the Lord through priests and offering animals, there is still a called-for sacrifice in order to know and understand the will of God for our lives. This sacrifice is our life devotion. Notice also the corresponding language in this scripture when compared to Malachi 3.

The Lord requires a sacrifice of consecration, that is holy and pure. This sacrifice is a life choice to forsake ourselves and live for Him. That is to say, we become true disciples of Christ, take up our cross and follow Him.

Paul spoke about an offering made by fire that is pleasing and acceptable, according to the Old Testament. There is namely something very pleasing to the Lord in the smell of burning flesh.

God Gave Cain an Opportunity to Repent

Notice, the Lord gave an opportunity for Cain to rectify the situation, warning him that if he chose rebellion, sin would be his master.

In order to walk in God's ordained authority on this earth and implement kingdom here as it is in heaven, He must be our master, not sin.

Pride Contaminates the Offering

It was Cain's pride that won in the end. Pride is the number one issue that defiles the offering. Therefore, pride is also the main area God deals with in His refiner's fire. It is when we try to do God's will our way, in our own strength and we are not surrendered under His leadership, authority and ways. Pride prevents us from yielding to the Lord's process and from entering the promises of God.

Hebrews 3:7-11

> *Therefore, as the Holy Spirit says: Today, if you will hear His voice, Do not harden your hearts, as [happened] in the rebellion [of Israel] and their provocation and embitterment [of Me] in the day of testing in the wilderness, Where your fathers tried [My patience] and tested [My forbearance] and found I stood their test, and they saw My works for forty years. And so I was provoked (displeased and sorely grieved) with that generation, and said, They always err and are led astray in their hearts, and they have not received or recognised My ways and become progressively better and more experimentally and intimately acquainted with them. Accordingly, I swore in My wrath and indignation, They shall not enter into My rest.*

Hardening our hearts is a result of resisting the process of God. Here the Lord says that He tested them in the wilderness and led them through in order to humble them.

Romans 4:16 states that the promises of God are inherited by faith and depend entirely on faith. Joshua and Caleb were the only two who believed God was able to do what He had promised. They didn't resist the process, but rather drew closer to Him in the wilderness. Joshua would wait outside the tabernacle of meeting when Moses went inside and after coming out, Joshua would go in to lay in the glory (Exodus 33:11).

Abraham, known as the father of faith, still made mistakes. He tried to fulfil God's promise of becoming the father of many nations through Ishmael. In Genesis 17:18, Abraham went to God and asked, "Oh that Ishmael might live before You!" This sounds similar to Cain. Won't You accept the works of my own hands?

Finally, we can ask ourselves the following questions again. Who will endure the day of His coming? Who wants to maintain status quo? Who desires to remain in control? Who wishes to stay bound and stuck in the pain of past traumas, wounds and bondages? Who will save their life, protect their reputation and place their confidence and reliance on earthly securities? Let our prayer be like David's.

Psalm 51:10 (KJV)

> *Create in me a clean heart, oh God; and renew a right spirit within me.*

Let Him kiss you with the kisses of His mouth. Pursue His heart and presence and allow His fire to refine you as silver and gold, reflecting redemption and His glory.

Chapter 5:

THE DAY OF THE LORD

Kingdom Day Is Coming

Late 2019, I had a dream where I saw a calendar. I noticed there were two days to go and on the third day I heard a BOOMING voice that said, "KINGDOM DAY IS COMING!"

It was very similar to my "Day of Ruach" dream where two days had passed and we were coming into the third day. Interestingly, the Lord used the words kingdom *day* is coming, instead of the kingdom is coming, which draws attention to the kingdom era rather than just the kingdom. Kingdom speaks of a state or country ruled by a king or queen, a realm under the control of a particular person or thing and refers also to the spiritual reign or authority of God.[46]

The Lord was declaring in my dream the coming of His kingdom on the third day which would establish His reign and government on the earth. This is the reign of the third day church. Ruling and reigning is a term used for those

---

46 www.lexico.com/definition/kingdom, accessed 12/01/2021

who have authority to legislate. They have authority to put into action and enforce the laws of the kingdom. Another term for this concept is dominion.

Dominion according to Merriam Webster dictionary is defined as: supreme authority, sovereignty or control, absolute ownership.[47]

The God-given birthright of believers is absolute ownership and supreme authority on the earth, which has been restored through the new covenant. This was man's first authorized position when created.

Genesis 1:26 (NKJV)

> Then God said, "Let Us make man in Our image, according to Our likeness; let them have **dominion** over the fish of the sea, over the birds of the air, and over the cattle, over all the earth and over every creeping thing that creeps on the earth. (emphasis mine)

Strong's Concordance defines *dominion* in the Hebrew as: to tread down, subjugate, prevail, rule over[48]

The Day Of The Lord

Malachi chapter four reveals kingdom day, the "day of the Lord" as the day that shall burn like an oven. This is when the people of God are operating in the fullness of kingdom governmental capacity, the sons of God are made manifest and are walking in dominion as described in Romans 8:19. They will *prevail, tread down* and *subjugate* the enemy.

---

47   www.merriam-webster.com/dictionary/dominion. Accessed 12/01/2021
48   James Strong. Strong's Expanded Exhaustive Concordance of the Bible (Nashville: Thomas Nelson, 2009), s.v *"dominion"*

Malachi 4:1-3

> *FOR BEHOLD,* **the day** *comes that shall burn like an oven, and all the proud and arrogant, yes, and all that do wickedly and are lawless, shall be stubble; the day that comes shall burn them up, says the Lord of hosts, so that it will leave them neither root nor branch. But unto you who revere and worshipfully fear My name shall the Sun of Righteousness arise with healing in His wings and His beams, and you shall go forth and gambol like calves [released] from the stall and leap for joy. And you shall* **tread down** *the lawless and the wicked, for they shall be ashes under the soles of your feet in the day that I shall do this, says the Lord of Hosts. (emphasis mine)*

Noteworthily, one of the meanings of dominion in Hebrew is to "tread down" which indicates the enemies of God being under the feet of His people. Furthermore, the victory and dominion over the wicked and the lawless is portrayed as ashes. We know that fire causes ashes. So when the sons of God are revealed and "released" like calves from the stall, they will be walking in a presence and fire of God that will burn up the lawlessness and wickedness of the enemy.

Ephesians 6:12 states that the wrestle is not with flesh and blood. In other words, humanity is not the enemy, but rather principalities and rulers of darkness in heavenly places, which are the lawless and the wicked noted in Malachi 4:3.

So how are the lawless and the wicked tread down and how do they become ashes under the feet of God's people, if the fight is not against flesh and blood?

In Matthew 16:19, Jesus tells His disciples:

> *I will give you the keys of the kingdom of heaven; and whatever you bind (declare to be improper and unlawful) on earth must be what is already bound in heaven; and whatever you loose (declare lawful) on earth must be what is already loosed in heaven.*

The keys that the Lord was referring to is the key of David as disclosed in Isaiah 22:22

> *And the key of the house of David I will lay upon his shoulder; he shall open and no one shall shut, he shall shut and no one shall open.*

Keys represent authority and ownership. When Jesus said in Matthew 16:19 that He has given His Church the keys to the kingdom, it signified authority and ownership of the kingdom. For instance, when you buy a house or car, you cannot use or access them without keys. Thus, you have no ownership or access if you do not possess keys. Additionally, keys are used to lock and unlock. Therefore, we as believers have the authority to unlock and release the kingdom of heaven on this earth and likewise lock up the kingdom of darkness. Unlocking the kingdom of heaven on earth means to release the operation and dominion of kingdom in that particular situation, and locking would look like denying access and shutting down the enemy's kingdom from operating in a situation. By Jesus giving the key of David to His people, He has enabled us to open and close gates or access points on earth. Believers have access to the authority and dominion of the kingdom of heaven and can govern earth as it is in heaven. As we are now seated in heavenly places with Christ (Ephesians 2:6), we don't govern from an earthly place or perspective. Jesus is the ancient eternal door spoken of in Psalm 24:9 that is the access to the King of Glory coming in. Who is the King of Glory? In my book "The Avenger – The Rise of the Kingdom", I extensively explain who the King of Glory is and what His coming looks like. In short, the King of Glory is the man of war who makes every wrong right, subdues nations and brings vengeance upon His enemies. He releases His might, justice and vengeance on earth through His church. The King of Glory is the full dominion of God revealed which is the Glory of His Kingdom. We as sons are to release and govern in the Glory of His Kingdom from the eternal realm where Christ is enthroned. Revelation 18:3 discloses that the Lamb's book of life existed before the foundation of the earth which is the eternal realm where Christ is, it is therefore not bound to the *chronos* time here on earth. *Chronos* is the Greek word used for the time and space we are governed by on earth. These are the hours, days, years and seasons that are steered by the sun and the moon. To bring heaven on earth, we step into the eternal realm, through Christ who was and is and is to come, and govern according to the mind of God (the Lord's original intent) concerning all things. We bring heaven on earth as we agree and partner with God's will and purposes that have been set and ordained by Him outside of *chronos* time. We are unable to reign from an earthly, *chronos* bound perspective and must position ourselves in the victory already achieved through Jesus, superimposing that victory *on earth as it is in heaven*. Furthermore, heaven's realm is victorious, pure, undefiled and whole. We gain access to this realm through Jesus and are instructed by Him to release this realm on earth. Simply stated, we are to release heaven's solutions over every situation or person void of the victory of the cross.

In Matthew 16:19, Jesus explains how to use these keys and govern by declarations in accordance with the Word of God.

> *I will give you the keys of the kingdom of heaven; and whatever you bind **(declare to be improper and unlawful)** on earth must be what is already bound in heaven; and whatever you loose **(declare lawful)** on earth must be what is already loosed in heaven. (emphasis mine)*

The keys to the kingdom in fact represent dominion on earth through *declarations.* As His people declare the Word of the Lord from their mouths, they are using the keys to open and close. He says to declare unlawful on earth those things that are unlawful in heaven. Jeremiah 23:29 states that the *Word* of God is like fire that burns up all that cannot endure the test.

Malachi 4:3 unfolds the meaning of *lawless*, stating that His people shall tread upon the lawless and the wicked and that they shall be ashes under their feet. In simple terms, whatever is unlawful in heaven shall become ashes under their feet by declaring the Word of the Lord from their mouths.

Hebrews 10:12-13 mentions that when Christ had offered Himself as a single sacrifice for our sins, He took His place at the right hand of the Father. There He waits until His enemies are made His footstool. Any time the term underfoot is mentioned in scripture it points to authority, dominion and victory. Another example can be found in Romans 16:20, *And the God of peace will soon crush Satan under your feet.* Notice both of these scripture references in Hebrews and Romans use future tense, expressing a time coming.

Kingdom Dominion

Psalm 110 speaks of the Day of the Lord's power, where the Lord will judge the earth, release the sons of God and make His enemies His footstool. This is the DAY OF THE LORD

Psalm 110:1

> *The Lord (God) says to my Lord (the Messiah), Sit at My right hand, until I make Your adversaries Your footstool.*

The verse above is revealing the day that He will make His enemies His footstool. The next verses describe what that day will look like.

Vs 2

> *The Lord will send forth from Zion the scepter of Your strength; rule, then, in the midst of Your foes.*

Candace Lucey suggests that Zion displays a temporal and spiritual image according to scripture. The temporal depiction is the city of Jerusalem where David ruled as king, the Davidic establishment (2 Samuel 5:7), whereas the spiritual portrayal is *the place God is enthroned* (Psalm 2:6). [49]

In Psalm 110:1 David was given insight into a conversation where the Father is inviting the Son to take His seat alongside Him. It seems David received a sneak peek of how the future Messianic Kingdom would look like, established upon David's throne.

Isaiah 9:6-7 (NKJV)

> *For unto us a Child is born, Unto us a Son is given; And the government will be upon His shoulder. And His name will be called Wonderful, Counselor, Mighty God, Everlasting Father, Prince of Peace. Of the increase of His government and peace There will be no end,* **Upon the throne of David** *and over His kingdom, To order it and establish it with judgement and justice. From that time forward, even forever. The zeal of the Lord of hosts will perform this. (emphasis mine)*

To understand this in context, the Zion referred to in Psalm 110:2 is not the literal Jerusalem but the spiritual structure of Zion – the Messianic kingdom of God established within His people. This spiritual picture of Zion, the place where the Lord is enthroned, involves new covenant people who have Christ as their King, Lord and Saviour. It is from this Zion that the body of believers, who have Christ enthroned in their hearts, will govern with the scepter of His kingdom.

---

49   Candace Lucey, "What is the Meaning of Zion in the Bible?", Christianity.com, July 03 2019, www.christianity.com/wiki/bible/what-is-the-meaning-of-zion-in-the-bible.html

A scepter is defined as a ceremonial staff, symbolizing power often used by kings.[50] It is also a symbol of the Lord's power, authority and rule. A key foundational precept of the kingdom government blueprint is that those with Christ enthroned in their hearts (Zion) will govern with the scepter of His kingdom. We could ask the question, "What do people with Christ enthroned in their hearts look like?" They are people walking in covenant, in full surrender to the authority and lordship of Christ, the Lord is their boss, the captain of the host.

Yes Sir – The Governmental Foundation Of Obedience

Early 2020, the Lord spoke to me in a dream where He was the Captain of the Hosts and He was calling His people into position as in an army. There was an urgency in His voice suggesting He was about to signal a command which would launch them into battle. This battle could be what the respected prophet Rick Joyner has addressed multiple times in his written work. The book "Army of the Dawn" relays Rick's prophetic insight into this great end time army. He writes;

> *This age will conclude with the ultimate battle between light*
> *and darkness. It will be the final confrontation between truth*
> *and lies, righteousness and wickedness, justice and injustice.*
> *It has been raging in every generation and in every place,*
> *but it will soon culminate in the ultimate clash of good and*
> *evil. The end of this age is near, and as this last battle is*
> *unfolding, everyone on earth must choose sides. There will*
> *be no neutral countries and be no neutral people.[51]*

Upon waking, I pondered this dream of mine and sought the Lord regarding the message He was trying to convey. I said, "What does this positioning look like Lord?" As I continued to press into the Lord, the Holy Spirit spoke to my heart loud and clear saying, "It's time for my people to learn how to say

50   Vocabulary.com, www.vocabulary.com/dictionary/scepter
51   Joyner, Army of the Dawn, 14,15.

"YES SIR"! This implies complete obedience to His voice. If Christ is truly enthroned in your life, then full obedience to His Lordship will follow.

In the military, knowing how to obey orders from superior officers in a battle situation is a matter of life and death. Success in any mission can be the direct result of this one factor.

When the Lord said to me, "My people need to learn how to say "YES SIR", I understood full surrender to His authority would be needed in His end time army in order to secure success in the mission. Alignment was needed within the ranks. Many needed to come into their rank and file position. Instead of doing their own thing and pursuing their own agendas, the Lord was calling His people back into alignment so they could be empowered with His governmental power to secure victory over the god of this world and make the Lord's enemies His footstool.

John Bevere so eloquently brings to our attention in His book "Under Cover", that before Adam and Eve's disobedience there were no fruits of corruption within mankind such as hatred, anger, unforgiveness, strife, gossip, fraud, bitterness, sexual perversion, drunkenness, murder, or theft.[52]

Therefore, it was the direct act of disobedience that opened the door to corruption. In this modern age, Christians are tempted to justify their partial obedience. However, the Lord throughout His word is very clear on the matter. Partial obedience is disobedience. One example that comes to mind where the Lord displayed gross displeasure to partial obedience is found in the book of 1 Samuel 15. King Saul was commanded by the Lord to *utterly* destroy Amalek as a display of God's vengeance upon their ancient sin towards Israel in the days of their escape from Egypt. He was told by God not to spare any person or livestock. However, Saul did not obey the Lord's command in its entirety. He spared the best of the livestock and kept alive the Amalekite king. When met by the prophet Samuel, Saul boasted of his achievements, declaring he had fulfilled the Lord's commandment. Samuel grieved in spirit because of

---

52   Bevere, Under Cover, 43,44.

Saul's disobedience asked why he could still hear the bleating of sheep and the lowing of oxen. Saul then blamed the people, explaining that they had saved the animals to sacrifice unto the Lord. Infuriated by Saul's stubbornness of heart, Samuel asked Saul why he did not obey the Lord in his mission against the Amalekites. Saul's response is mindboggling. He said in 1 Samuel 15:20-21 (NKJV),

> *And Saul said to Samuel, "But I have obeyed the voice of the Lord, and gone on the mission on which the Lord sent me, and brought back Agag king of Amalek; I have utterly destroyed the Amalekites. But the people took of the plunder, sheep and oxen, the best of the things which should have been utterly destroyed, to sacrifice to the Lord your God in Gilgal".*

Saul honestly thought that because he almost obeyed the voice of the Lord, it equalled complete obedience. He assumed he could pick some parts of God's command to obey and disregard the other parts by doing his own thing. Saul was even bold enough to declare his partial obedience as a righteous act as if he knew better than God! In this case God did not ask for the sacrifice, he required obedience. Samuel gobsmacked at Saul's hardness of heart and lack of reverence, prophesied one of the most famous passages in scripture.

1 Samuel 15:22-23

> *Samuel said: "Has the Lord as great a delight in burnt offerings and sacrifices as in obeying the voice of the Lord? Behold, to obey is better than sacrifice, and to hearken than the fat of rams. For rebellion is as the sin of witchcraft, and stubbornness is as idolatry and teraphim (household good luck images). Because you have rejected the word of the Lord, He also has rejected you from being king".*

The displeasure of the Lord was clearly kindled against Saul because of his direct disobedience. Even though Saul tried to justify his partial obedience as noble, the Lord called it rebellion. Good intentions do not please God. Paul teaches in Romans 14:23 that whatever does not originate from faith is sin. This means that whatever is not within the boundaries of God's instruction is outright rebellion, there is no middle ground. The consequences of Saul's partial obedience were dire. After Samuel addressed Saul's disobedience, Saul tried to retract from his consequence without repentance. He admitted that it was fear of man that caused him to disobey the Lord, but didn't repent within that space. He continued to try and save face and retain honour before the people by asking Samuel to return with him to worship the Lord before Israel. As Samuel turned from Saul, Saul seized the skirt of Samuel's garment and it tore. And Samuel said to him, *"The Lord has torn the kingdom of Israel from you this day and has given it to a neighbor of yours who is better than you"* (1 Samuel 15:28). In that moment, Saul was disqualified from his governmental seat. If disobedience disqualified a king from government, then obedience is imperative to operate in the authority of kingdom government. Saul was a hypocrite. God will not entrust the authority of His kingdom to imposters. Today, the house of Saul could be likened to the religious systems and traditions of man which are not yielded and surrendered to the leading of the Lord. David, however was a man after God's own heart and upon his throne the Lord established His messianic rule (Isaiah 9:7).

Obedience doesn't always feel good. It can be extremely uncomfortable for the flesh. It comes down to whether or not you are seeking to please the Father or yourself.

James 3:16 (NKJV)

> For where envy and **self-seeking** exist, confusion and every
> evil thing are there. (emphasis mine)

Chaos and confusion are direct results of rebellion. An army that is ruled by rebellion will be dominated by chaos and confusion. In order to function in smooth sequence, with clarity, vision and purpose, those called to the Lord's army must be empty of selfish ambition and rivalry. This ancient evil, must be eliminated from a believer's heart to possess victory.

Consecration – The Beauty Of Holiness

David was given insight as to how the Lord would make His enemies His footstool. The Lord's people would rule and reign from Zion with the scepter of His kingdom and in turn governmental power would be released on this earth. Psalm 110 continues,

Vs 3

> *Your people will offer themselves willingly in the day of Your power,....*

The day of the Lord brings forth a people willing to offer themselves as a living sacrifice unto the Lord (Romans 12:1). This is the foundational quality and precedent to operating in full kingdom government power. Revelation 12:11 (KJV) is explicitly forthright regarding the essential standard of overcoming people.

> *And they overcame him by the blood of the Lamb, and by the word of their testimony; and they loved not their lives unto the death.*

Three specific ingredients are clarified here for believers who desire to walk in an overcoming lifestyle. The third being loving not one's life even unto death. In Psalm 110:3, David articulates so beautifully his vision of these overcoming people so consecrated unto the Lord.

> *....in the beauty of holiness and in holy array out of the womb of the morning: to You [will spring forth] Your young men, who are as the dew.*

The word *holiness*, according to Strong's Concordance translates in the Hebrew as: a sacred place or thing, sanctity: consecrated, dedicated, hallowed, holiness.[53]

Brown-Driver-Briggs' definition of *holiness* is: to be set apart and separate[54]

Holiness is beautiful. People who have been consecrated unto the Lord and do not possess mixture, reflect the beauty of God. Strong's Concordance translates the word *beauty* as: splendour, majesty, magnificence[55]

The Lord endows His set apart, consecrated people with His majesty, splendour and magnificence. The next part of this verse says that from the *womb of the morning* will come forth the young men. This speaks of the dawning of the new day giving birth to the sons of God, and despite their age they will come forth with the strength of young men which includes women as well. We are all one in Christ, there is neither male nor female (Galatians 3:28).

This new morning is the third day, where the sons of God are made manifest. Zion is their habitation where Christ is enthroned in their hearts. They are consecrated and set apart unto the Lord, arrayed in His splendour and resurrection power, ruling with the scepter of His kingdom, making His enemies His footstool.

---

53   James Strong. Strong's Expanded Exhaustive Concordance of the Bible
       (Nashville: Thomas Nelson, 2009), s.v *"holiness"*
54   Enhanced Brown-Driver-Briggs Hebrew and English Lexicon, Clarendon Press, 1977 *"holiness"*
55   James Strong. Strong's Expanded Exhaustive Concordance of the Bible
       (Nashville: Thomas Nelson, 2009), s.v *"beauties"*

Chapter 6:

OVERCOMERS GOVERN IN THE FEAR OF THE LORD

In addition to the principles of consecration and obedience, the fear of the Lord is another foundational prerequisite to governing in kingdom authority and dominion.

The Fear Of The Lord — Divine Order Of Kingdom Government

"Before God's Glory comes, there first must be divine order"[56]

Divine order represents God's ways. God doesn't operate within the limitations and systems of man's ways, although mankind has been subject to this thinking in the past. The Lord is restoring His divine order with a view to re-establish His people into kingdom governmental power.

---

56   Bevere, The Fear of the Lord. 31

Isaiah 11:1-4

AND THERE shall come forth a Shoot out of the stock of Jesse [David's father], and a Branch out of his roots shall grow and bear fruit.

*And the Spirit of the Lord shall rest upon Him - the Spirit of wisdom and understanding, the Spirit of counsel and might, the Spirit of knowledge and of the **reverential and obedient fear of the Lord**–*

*And shall make Him of quick understanding, and His delight shall be in the **reverential and obedient fear of the Lord**, And He shall not judge by the sight of His eyes, neither decide by the hearing of His ears;*

But with righteousness and justice shall He judge the poor and decide with fairness for the meek, the poor, and the downtrodden of the earth; and He shall smite the earth and the oppressor with the rod of His mouth, and with the breath of His lips He shall slay the wicked. (emphasis mine)

The abovementioned scripture reveals the precepts and precedents of Messiah's reign and as He is, so are His saints in the world (1 John 4:17). God's people who are seated in heavenly places with Christ, and share His same governmental capacity, are to govern according to the divine order of the Messianic establishment which is encapsulated in the fear of the Lord.

The Fear Of The Lord –
Governing In The Counsel Of God

Isaiah 11:1-4 also portrays the fear of the Lord as indispensable to governing according to the wisdom of God instead of carnal reasoning – *And He shall not judge by the sight of His eyes, neither decide by the hearing of His ears.* This statement acknowledges complete submission to the Father and His ways and suggests access to the counsel of God. It is by the fear of the Lord that one is connected to His counsel. Notice that He couples counsel with the word *might* which is His power and strength. His Word and power are joined together in ruling and reigning. The counsel of God refers to His decrees and declarations over a situation, which is how the saints also govern over regions, nations, families or any other sphere of influence they have been assigned to. Believers govern by the counsel of God through the fear of the Lord. What is God saying over issues, situations and problems? What is His will in heaven that needs to be released on earth? Too often in prayer, people decree their own will on earth and declare what they want, expecting God to bless it. God is commonly treated as a genie, whom they use to bless their own desires. This attitude has developed a weak church which lacks governmental authority and power.

This lack of the fear of God is what causes His people to treat Him like a genie or a Mr. Fix it, rather than seeking His face for His will, purposes and plans. After being in the ministry for over twenty years, I have unfortunately observed a gross lack of the fear of the Lord among the saints. Some only come to God when they want Him to do or fix something for them. They don't spend time with Him or speak to Him for weeks on end, and then when they need something or experience calamity they expect God to just show up and give the solution.

Proverbs 1:27-30

> *When your panic comes as a storm and desolation and your calamity comes on as a whirlwind, when distress and anguish come upon you. Then will they call upon me [Wisdom] but I will not answer; they will seek me early and diligently but they will not find me. Because they hated knowledge and **did not choose the reverent and worshipful fear of the Lord**, would accept none of my **counsel**, and despised all my **reproof**. (emphasis mine)*

Some only want the counsel of God when it makes them feel good and is what they desire to hear. But God says here in Proverbs 1:27-30 that His counsel also includes reproof and correction. To love knowledge, accept the Lord's counsel and receive His reproof, is to choose the fear of the Lord. The scripture mentioned above stresses that the fear of the Lord is chosen. People can reject the fear of the Lord, and in the day of calamity they will not be able to find the wisdom from the counsel of heaven for their situation. They are like the foolish virgins in Matthew 25 that are unprepared because they have relied on their own insight. In the hour of need they go to those who have been prepared, have walked in the fear of God and have eyes to see in the midst of darkness. Unfortunately, there is not enough oil for them both to burn the candle of vision and the unwise virgin must go away and buy for herself. In order to gain access to the counsel, the Word and the instruction of God, the fear of the Lord must be present in one's life. He is God Almighty, the all awesome and magnificent one, Creator of the heavens and earth and deserves to be served in reverence and awe.

In some ways, the church have behaved like King Saul and have chosen disobedience, the fear of man and rebellion, but when in trouble they seek the counsel of the Lord as if consulting a magician. Saul consulted a medium to call up the dead prophet Samuel to seek counsel from God in his hour of trouble (1 Samuel 28). Saul knew that this was an abomination to the Lord (Deuteronomy 18:10-12). He had banished from Israel all mediums and those who practiced witchcraft and for that reason he had to find one outside of Israel. Saul wanted to access the oracle or counsel of God outside of the precedents of God. Sadly, many in the body of Christ are like Saul and don't understand God's ways in operating in victory and power. In many ways, Saul's style of leadership has kept God's people stunted in their maturity in Christ. It's time for God's people to grow up into sonship and start using the keys to the kingdom, declaring what is lawful and unlawful and governing in the realm of the spirit via the counsel of God.

This example of Saul, is a sober reminder to God's people that without the fear of the Lord one operates in carnal reasoning and selfish ambition, and enters the spirit realm through another door. It is not acceptable to play the harlot one week and then approach God the next week as if He is a genie who fixes troubles. One must understand God's divine order and operate in the fear of the Lord.

Wisdom – The Key To Governing By His Spirit

Proverbs 15:33

> *The reverent and worshipful fear of the Lord brings instruction in Wisdom, and humility comes before honor.*

When people submit to the fear of the Lord, their eyes and ears are open to His counsel, will and wisdom regarding the situation. They understand which strategies need to be implemented and release those answers by decrees and declarations. At times they are to act and obey an instruction by faith to bring kingdom, just as Joshua did in Jericho. But if Joshua did not yield to the counsel and instruction of heaven brought to him by the warrior angel, he would not have had the victory in Jericho. Joshua could have lacked the fear of God and said, "No, I am not going to do that. I'm not marching around those walls. We will all look like ridiculous, crazy people instead of strong, fearsome warriors! I mean who does that? Walking around a wall for seven days and on the seventh day, seven times! Then to shout and blow the trumpets and gain victory? Goodness, Lord!" There could have been a temptation to modify the instructions in order to preserve dignity and reputation. However, Joshua knew true victory came through believing and acting upon the strategy and counsel of God. The saints are to govern in the same manner by the fear of the Lord in obedience to His counsel and instruction. From this posture, the authority and government of heaven is released through His people.

Proverbs 9:10a (NKJV)

The fear of the Lord is the beginning of wisdom

Isaiah 11:2 revealed that the spirit of wisdom and understanding would rest upon Messiah to govern along with the reverential fear of the Lord.

Godly wisdom is not man's intelligence and it is not even comparable. Human intelligence is fallible and limited, but the wisdom of God truly brings heaven on earth. John 8:1-11 paints a picture of Jesus governing in the wisdom of God, which saved a woman's life. A woman was caught in adultery and according to the law of Moses her punishment was death by stoning. The Pharisees and scribes brought her to Jesus and asked Him His judgment on the situation with the intention of testing and consequently accusing Him. Jesus not answering them, began to write in the sand. As they continued to press Him for a response, Jesus stood and asked for the person without sin to cast the first stone at her. This wise response convicted the woman's accusers, causing them to retreat and depart from the scene. Jesus then asked the woman where her accusers were and she said there were none. Neither did Jesus condemn her, but instead admonished her to sin no more. It was the wisdom of God that prevailed and delivered her from death, more importantly she received forgiveness of sin and the path of repentance was revealed.

If Jesus feared man, He would have bowed to the pressures to save His own reputation and deliver this woman up to her accusers. There was pressure from the Pharisees to ensnare Him and trip Him up. However, it was the fear of the Lord that enabled Him to govern in wisdom in this situation. Reiterating

Isaiah 11:3b, He did not judge this scenario by the sight of His eyes, neither did He decide the case by the hearing of His ears. If Jesus had been influenced by what He saw and heard about this women, He would not have been able to access the counsel of God and release the righteous "judgement" in this situation.

The Fear Of The Lord Holds
A Standard Of Righteousness

Isaiah 11:4 states that with *righteous* judgements the Lord will make decisions. People walking in the fear of God are governed by *righteousness* not ruled by *need.*

The Amplified Classic Bible describes one meaning of *righteousness* as doing Christianity God's way.

Matthew 6:33

> *But seek (aim at and strive after) first of all His kingdom and His righteousness* **(His way of doing and being right)**, *and then all these things taken together will be given you besides. (emphasis mine)*

People walking in the fear of the Lord are those who desire to operate in God's ways. But those driven by need will compromise God's way to satisfy the need.

Hosea 2:5

> *For their mother has played the harlot; she who conceived them has done shamefully, for she said, I will go after my lovers that give me my food and my water, my wool and my flax, my oil and my refreshing drinks.*

Hosea is describing a people who have compromised righteousness for need. They have forsaken the ways of God for earthly carnal needs. Harlotry is for gain. It is the exchange of a need for a service.

The Lord is challenging His people in this time on the eve of the second day, to rid their temple of all the idols they have put before Him as their source, all compromises and everything that has stood in the way of their relationship with God.

Scripture exhorts the saints to seek *first* the Kingdom of God and His righteousness and all things will be added unto them (Matthew 6:33).

God's kingdom is heaven's answers to His people's needs, it's heaven's way, governmental order, justice and judgment, not man's wisdom.

Those who walk in governmental authority in the fear of the Lord place God's ways first regardless of their earthly lot. They are not governed by need but by righteousness.

Proverbs 14:14 (NKJV)

> *A backslider in heart will be filled with his own ways, But a good man will be satisfied from above.*

People of covenant are satisfied from above. They are not filled with their own ways but seek to do life God's way and the Lord will entrust them with His governmental authority. They will not fold under pressure to compromise because of persecution, but will stand strong in their faith, when it is put to the test.

Overcomers Govern In The Fear Of The Lord

Proverbs 14:26a

In the reverent and worshipful fear of the Lord there is strong confidence

Strong's concordance translates the word *strong* as: strength, boldness, power and might.[57]

The word *confidence* according to Strong's Concordance translates as: hope, surety, trust, assurance.[58]

When the saints are operating in the fear of the Lord, they are walking in boldness, power and might, all the while being full of hope, trust and assurance in God. These are all governmental attributes that characterize an overcomer.

The First Mention Of The Fear Of The Lord – A Foundation Of Faith

The principle of faith is also a necessary component of an overcoming church. Hebrews 11:1 explains that faith is the *assurance* of the things hoped for, the evidence of things not seen. Interestingly, one of the Hebrew meanings of confidence in Proverbs 14:26 is *assurance*. The fear of the Lord is an environment where faith operates in its purest form. In fact, the first mention of the fear of the Lord in scripture was when Abraham demonstrated faith in its highest measure by offering Isaac unto the Lord on Mt Moriah.

---

57   James Strong. Strong's Expanded Exhaustive Concordance of the Bible
      (Nashville: Thomas Nelson, 2009), s.v *"strong"*
58   Ibid., *"confidence"*

Genesis 22:12

> *And He said, Do not lay your hand on the lad or do anything to him;* **for now I know that you fear and revere God***, since* **you have not held back from Me** *or begrudged giving Me your son, your only son. (emphasis mine)*

Abraham held nothing back from God. The promise of God was not even an idol. Abraham's act of faith declared that nothing could come between his relationship and obedience to God. This pleased God and the Lord provided the ram for the sacrifice. Right after the first mention of the fear of the Lord in Genesis 22:12, the Lord provided the ram for Abraham's sacrifice instead of Isaac and revealed Himself for the first time as Jehovah Jireh. The "God who sees to it", which means the God who will see to your needs, He will provide.

Genesis 22:14 (KJV)

> *And Abraham called the name of that place Jehovah-Jireh: as it is said to this day, In the mount of the Lord it shall be seen.*

This is what a covenant relationship looks like in the fear of the Lord.

The Fear Of Man Versus The Fear Of The Lord

> *"If you desire the praise of man, you will fear man. If you fear man, you will serve him – for you will serve what you fear".[59]*

When man's ways are promoted, God's ways are denied. When God's ways are denied and are not honoured, people step into a very dangerous place in Christianity. This is a space void of the fear of the Lord.

---

59   Bevere, The Fear of the Lord. 67

With the exaltation of religion these last two thousand years, one main ingredient to kingdom government has been lacking at large, and that is the FEAR OF THE LORD. The Fear of the Lord is a governmental foundation. Without it present in the life of a believer, authority and power will be non-existent.

In systems of religion and tradition, man's needs are preferred and honoured before the desire to please God. The desire to please man over God is called the "fear of man". A person can only fear one of the two. They will either fear man, or God. Fear of man is self-focused, whereas the fear of God is God-focused.

When people fear God they rest under His authority, but the fear of man will place them under man's control. People can only govern in the realm of authority they are submitted to. If God, then they have access to His authority, if man, then they are bound by the limitations of man's authority. Man's authority operating apart from God is seated in the carnal earthly realm of death, decay and corruption (Romans 8:6-7). This authority has no ability to bring any eternal and supernatural change or impact on this earth.

As discussed in the previous chapter, King Saul was rebuked by the prophet Samuel for utterly disrespecting the Word of the Lord in his act of rebellion. His disobedience and rebellion disqualified him from his governmental seat and the Lord vowed to give his kingdom to another better than him. The root of Saul's disobedience and lack of reverence for God's instruction is found in the following verse.

1 Samuel 15:24

> *And Saul said to Samuel, I have sinned; for I have transgressed the commandment of the Lord and your words, because **I feared the people and obeyed their voice**. (emphasis mine)*

Fear of any kind will seek to paralyze believers and lead them into self-preservation. Fearful people are selfish and ultimately untrustworthy.[60]

The Lord, therefore, tore the kingdom from Saul, because he could not be trusted with the authority and responsibility of governing God's people in righteousness. He lacked integrity and compromised the commandment of God at a hint of persecution. He was more concerned about what people thought of him than God. Fear of man, loss, death, conflict, rejection, are all driven by self-preservation. Those governed by fear, live for themselves and do whatever it takes to secure their own comfort. Faith, on the other hand, will cause believers to walk a path of denying themselves. It will lead them in the path of righteousness for His name sake, not their own. Saul was concerned with his own reputation. His governmental decisions were motivated from a place of self-preservation. Even after he had admitted his transgression, he still wanted to secure his reputation before the people by asking Samuel to go with him to worship the Lord before them (1 Samuel 15:25-31). Samuel was grieved because of Saul's unrepentant heart and deep need to salvage his reputation instead of truly being sorrowful over his sin.

Proverbs 29:25 (NKJV)

> *The fear of man brings a snare, But whoever trusts in the Lord shall be safe.*

The Strong's Concordance translates the word *snares* as: a noose for catching animals, a hook for the nose.[61]

Animals are usually caught by their captors in traps because of a need which is generally food. The enemy uses the same tactics with humanity. He entices people into a snare by using a need. One should ponder on this question: Which need exalts itself over the willingness to obey God? Is it the

---

60   Drew Linsalata, "EP1010 – The selfish nature of anxiety and fear" theanxioustruth.com, March 25, 2020, https://theanxioustruth.com/selfish-anxiety/
61   James Strong. Strong's Expanded Exhaustive Concordance of the Bible (Nashville: Thomas Nelson, 2009), s.v *"snare"*

need for man's approval, peace, joy, material things, recognition or control? If the Lord is the source to someone's needs, then that person will not be driven or ensnared by them. Thus, the fear of the Lord will set people free from being need-driven and compromising their faith.

Proverbs 16:6b

> *By the reverent, worshipful fear of the Lord men depart from and avoid evil.*

Those who have fear as their commander in chief are dangerous in a battle situation. They are incapable of obeying any command or instruction from the Lord. Instead of being governed by faith and trust in God, they will yield to the self-preserving voice of fear. Hence, why God purged Gideon's army of the fearful.

Judges 7:2-3

> *The Lord said to Gideon, the people who are with you are too many for Me to give the Midianites into their hands, lest Israel boast about themselves against Me, saying My own hand has delivered me. So now proclaim in the ears of the men saying,* **Whoever is fearful** *and trembling, let him turn back and depart from Mount Gilead. And 22,000 of the men returned, but 10,000 remained. (emphasis mine)*

Fear hinders the ability to operate in faith as it compromises a believer's love walk and capability to walk in power and operate in a sound mind.

2 Timothy 1:7 (NKJV)

> *For God has not given us a spirit of fear, but of power and of love and of a sound mind.*

Jesus said in order to walk in love and love your neighbour, it requires a laying down of your life for that person. However, a person full of fear will seek to save their own life first before the life of a brother. This is not just speaking of a physical life and death situation, but it could refer to various scenarios where people are tempted to put themselves first. Those governed by the fear of man, seek to save their own reputations over doing what is right. They would save face instead of being loyal and faithful to the Lord and their fellow brethren.

Fear can be a hidden enemy in the heart. It surfaces at the most crucial times when a battle could be won or lost. Peter the apostle was well acquainted with this hidden enemy of the heart. On the night Jesus was put on trial, Peter announced his undying allegiance, only to have Jesus inform him that before the cock crowed that night he would have denied Jesus three times (John 18:15-26). What caused Peter to deny Jesus? It was the fear of death. Peter was afraid he too would be put in chains and sentenced to death. However, the beauty in this story is that Peter eventually overcame fear that caused him to deny and compromise his faith and allegiance to the Lord. Peter became a martyr for Christ. He loved not his life even unto death. Even though Peter failed his first test, he eventually became the rock upon whom Jesus would build His church and the gates of hell would not prevail against it (Matthew 16:18). What does that mean? Peter was previously known as Simon. The name Simon means reed or to be soft and bendable.[62] Jesus however, said that he was to be called Peter which meant rock. He was proclaiming Peter's transformation from someone who easily caved under the pressure of persecution and fear of man to an unmovable, unshakeable person who would stand boldly for Christ. His solid and loyal faith would endure against the very gates of hell. This is the kind of faith that the Lord would build His church upon. This overcoming, victorious church does not fear what man could do to them but only fears the One with power over the body and soul (Matthew 10:28). These victorious ones who do not fear man, but God, build

---

62   Juan Rodriguez, "From Reed to Rock", thedefender.org, accessed 01/29/2020, http://www.thedefender.org/From%20Reed%20to%20Rock.html

their house on the rock which cannot be shaken or moved and endure until the end.

I once heard it said, "Faith is not the absence of fear."

This statement is true as proven in the story of Gideon. When the Lord called him while threshing wheat in the winepress (Judges 6), the angel of the Lord said to him in verse 23, *"Peace be to you, do not fear; you shall not die."* Obviously, Gideon was fearful for his life. The Lord also came to Joshua, a brave warrior of Israel, before leading them into the promised land and told him to be strong and of good courage (Joshua 1:6-7). The fear of man causes us as God's people to stumble and prevents us from overcoming and inheriting our God-given birthright. The fear of God, on the contrary, causes us to possess and operate in an overcoming faith that defies the impossible.

The Fear Of The Lord Brings The Restoration Of Glory

Psalm 85:9 (NKJV)

> *Surely His salvation is near to those who fear Him, That* **glory** *may dwell in our land. (emphasis mine)*

According to Strong's Concordance the word *salvation* translates from the Hebrew as: freedom, deliverance, liberty, prosperity, safety, victory.

In its root meaning it is defined as: wide and free, to defend, avenging, **bring salvation**[63]

The word *glory* in Hebrew according to the Strong's Concordance means: weight of God, splendour, glorious majesty.[64]

---

[63]   James Strong. Strong's Expanded Exhaustive Concordance of the Bible (Nashville: Thomas Nelson, 2009), s.v *"salvation"*
[64]   Ibid., *"glory"*

So, Psalm 85:9 discloses that people who fear God have access to victory, deliverance, freedom and prosperity and a platform is created for the Lord's glory, majesty and splendour to abide. In recent years the church has been crying out for revival. They have been interceding for the power of God to be made manifest in their midst. This scripture reveals the fear of the Lord as the divine order required for the glory to abide in the midst of His people, enabling the saints to walk in the new covenant fruits of freedom. The greater glory that the Lord is preparing His people for is a governmental authority. Glory according to this verse means weight. It is therefore a weighty governmental authority which demands great responsibility. People who walk in the fear of the Lord know how to operate in the weight of His majesty and do not misuse their authority for selfish gain.

The Fear Of God Is The Key To Revival

Proverbs 14:27 (KJV)

> *The fear of the Lord is a fountain of life, To depart from the snares of death.*

Strong's Concordance interprets the word *fountain* from the Hebrew text as: something dug, that is generally a source of water, a spring[65]

The word *life* is translated in the Strong's Concordance as: alive and in the root word it means: revive - to recover, restore, repair to save, to bring back to life.[66]

As discussed in chapter two, the root Hebrew word for *revive* in Hosea 6:2 is the same for the word *life* in Proverbs 14:27. The key then to being revived according to this scripture is a return to the fear of the Lord. As the church is praying for revival and awakening, a return to the fear of God is indispensable.

---

65   Ibid., *"fountain"*
66   Ibid., *"life"*

The second part of Proverbs 14:27 holds also some vital lessons.

> *The fear of the Lord is a fountain of life,* **To depart from the snares of death**. *(emphasis mine)*

The word *depart* according to Strong's Concordance is defined as: to turn off, to **decline**, revolt, rebel.[67]

Another meaning according to Brown-Driver-Briggs lexicon is to *avoid.*[68]

The fear of God is a fountain of life, meaning a life source which causes His people to be alive to God and led by the Spirit, furthermore preventing them from being need-driven due to Him being the number one source.

Notice that one of the words used to describe *depart* in Proverbs 14:27 is to "decline". I found this interpretation amusing when I pondered upon it. You can imagine the enemy seeking to tempt and allure God's people into sin or distraction and him being met with a simple "I decline" response. When God is your source, you can easily "decline" the temptations of the enemy.

Jeremiah calls the harlot church of Israel back to the fountain of life. He was in essence implying that they return to the fear of God and pursue Him as their source.

Jeremiah 2:13

> *For My people have committed two evils: they have forsaken Me, the Fountain of living waters, and they have hewn for themselves cisterns, broken cisterns which cannot hold water.*

Israel was no longer looking to the Lord as their source but chose an inferior and broken one that could not sustain or maintain life. Jesus said to

---

the Samaritan woman at the well in John 4 that if she drank from His living waters, she would never thirst again. The Lord is enough to sustain His people and is the only source needed to walk *in His likeness* and *by His Spirit*. How can people be led by His Spirit if they are drinking from another source? How can people hear the words of life if they are being sustained by another narrative (John 6:68)? In order to walk in the fear of the Lord and operate in the counsel and government of God, His people must have Him as their source of life and His words must be their final truth.

When we are not walking in the fear of the Lord, we are not aligned with His wisdom, and are therefore limited in our own understanding. Man can think in his own mind that he is clever, but in fact earthly wisdom lacks supernatural insight.

The Dawn Breakers – The End Time Overcoming Army Revealed In The Fear Of The Lord

In August of 2020 during a time of prophetic worship I went into an encounter with the Lord that evolved like the story of a movie.

Scene One: Christ Walking amongst the Lampstands (This is Where the Body of Christ is Now)

In this scene I was caught into a vision where Jesus was walking amongst the lampstands. I was in great awe and the fear of the Lord as I was beholding Him. He was fiery and serious. It was a holy atmosphere as He was searching intently amongst the lampstands for those who had filled their lamps. He held a torch of fire in his hand ready to light the lamps who were prepared and ready to burn for Him in this hour. In this moment I was reminded of a word He had been speaking to me regarding the time we are in, which is as follows:

Who has heard the call? Who has heard the call to prepare and trim their wicks? Who has heard the call to fill their lamps with oil? The trumpet blows in this hour for the church to assemble. There is a call to assemble, to hear the instructions from the Captain of the Hosts. But in order for His people to hear the new instruction, they must hear the trumpet that is calling them out, calling them into repentance, calling them into position to raise their arm and salute the King of Kings and say, "YES SIR!" There is a trumpet that is blowing from the mouths of the prophets to God's people to COME OUT!!! This is a call to come out from TWO places.

1. A CALL TO COME OUT FROM BABYLON
– The mixture of the world (Revelation 18:4).

2. A CALL TO COME OUT FROM SAUL'S HOUSE
– The mixture of religion, tradition and the pride of man-made systems.

The Lord gave me a dream in January 2020, with such an urgent message to tell His people to:

"GET OFF THE FENCE BECAUSE THE FIRE IS COMING!"

The fire of God will test and approve His house. It will fall and burn up the worldly mixture of Babylon that has infiltrated His house and it will burn up the religious systems of Saul's house. When God's fire comes, it burns up His enemies (Psalm 97:3). The Lord is going to burn up the enemies that have set themselves up in His house and have led His people astray. He told me in a dream in August 2019, that He is going to release a fire we have not yet seen. When it comes it consumes all that cannot endure the test, which is built on wood hay and straw (Malachi 3:2-3, 1 Corinthians 3:12-13).

The Lord is beckoning His people to come out of the mixture of the world, religion and tradition, which makes the Word of God of no effect (Revelation 18, Jeremiah 51, Mark 7:13).

The call to His people right now is to come out from the kingdoms that are built on wood, hay and straw and to abide in the kingdom of gold, silver and precious stones. This fire is going to expose and judge the corruption in His house that have been built on Babylonian systems (the world) and the religious systems (Saul's house). It will expose the perversion of Baal and the deceptions of Saul's leadership. Instead of repenting before the Lord for the fear of man and lack of the fear of God, Saul stooped further into sin by going to witchcraft for inspiration (1 Samuel 28). Witchcraft is works of the flesh (Galatians 5:19-21), and the fire of God is going to burn up the works of the flesh that have built a system around the praise of man rather than God. The Lord is going to deal with the Saul leadership in His house that have quenched the Spirit of God moving among His people, in order to build their own kingdoms and He is going to raise up Davids to take their place (1 Samuel 15:28). He will also challenge the Ahab leaders in His house that have tolerated mixture with the world, allowing the altar of the Lord to be polluted by the spirit of perversion. In their place He will anoint the Jehus who will UPROOT Baal out of the land (2 Kings 10:28).

The Fire of God, however, is good news for those who have their lamps filled, because it empowers the righteous to become bold witnesses upon the earth (Acts 1:8). The fire of God will promote and thrust forth those who have been wise virgins and have filled their lamps and trimmed their wicks in this last season. For as in the days of Elijah, the fire will land upon the altars of the righteous and reveal the Living God in their lives.

Scene 2: The Mantling of the Fear of the Lord

The next scene in this encounter was like a still moment. It felt like I was being cloaked by a swirling light. I knew it was not just me, but I represented those who had had their lamps lit in the previous scene. I asked the Lord what I was being mantled with because I knew I was receiving a new mantle. He said, "This is the FEAR OF THE LORD. This is what my people will need to OVERCOME."

The scene seemed to go on for a while, it was not a fleeting moment but a drenching, a new baptism, a moment of pause that was being mantled. I felt this will be a move of the Spirit of the Lord upon His beloved.

This move of the fear of the Lord, will mantle the Bride with governmental power. She will shift gears into the apostolic breaker of the THIRD DAY.

Scene 3: The Dawn Breakers – The Army of the New Day

As I was being clothed in light before entering the last scene of this encounter, there was a pause. I then saw gross darkness. But the Lord said "look toward the horizon". As I looked, I could see this shadow of a hill. Then the Lord said "watch and see" as He changed my position from the darkness to peering over the hill. He said "look what is coming" and my whole insides began to tremble, I felt like I was literally going to explode with the power, awe and even sense of dread at what I was beholding. It was a FIERCE ARMY. The Lord said "Here they come! The DAWN BREAKERS. They are the ones who will break through the darkness. Look and see My Glory is rising on them, My Glory will be seen on them. Nations will come through them to the light. The light on them is the rising of the dawn and they will bring forth the new day. They are the VICTORIOUS ONES, the OVERCOMERS, this is the ARMY OF THE NEW DAY."

Malachi 4 prophesies "the day of the Lord", the day His people will operate in their birthright of governmental power.

The scripture says in Malachi 4:2-3

> *But unto you who revere and worshipfully Fear My name, shall the Sun of Righteousness arise with healing in His wings and His beams, and you shall go forth and gambol like calves [released] from the stall and leap for joy. And you shall tread down the lawless and the wicked, for they shall be*

ashes under the soles of your feet in the day I shall do this,
says the Lord of Hosts.

In this passage of scripture, the Lord signs off as the "Lord of Hosts", meaning the captain of hosts, the man of war, the captain of the army, which is war talk. This is, thus, the coming forth of the overcoming ARMY OF THE LORD.

Satanic kingdoms and lawless, wicked establishments will be ashes under the soles of their feet. They will walk in the very fire of His presence that burns up the Lord's enemies, as they are ones who minister before the very throne of God. They are not mixed with the wine of the world, nor do they play the harlot. These burning ones have endured the day of the Lord's coming and have yielded to the refiner's fire (Malachi 3:3), which purified them of selfish, need-driven desires of the heart; now wholly committed in love and allegiance to their king.

Notice as well in verse 2 of Malachi 4 the phrase, "FOR THOSE WHO FEAR MY NAME". So after the mantling of the fear of the Lord, the mighty ones will arise with the light (Sun of Righteousness) on them, which will break through the dawn and call forth the NEW DAY. They will carry the fire and the glory, and they will cause His enemies to be His footstool.

Chapter 7:

HUMILITY THE POSITION OF GOVERNMENTAL POWER

The Government Of God Cannot Rest Upon Man-Made Systems

As discussed earlier, the Lord has given His people the keys to the kingdom, but throughout the ages, the church has replaced the keys of government with religious systems. Consequently, causing intimacy to be replaced by formulas and traditions, and made-made systems to take the place of true spiritual authority. Sadly, these systems of man have hindered His people from being led by the Spirit, which is the original blueprint for their God-given authority and dominion.

The leading of the Spirit originates from intimacy and relationship, not from rules, regulations or systems of man. Religion and tradition exalt man's agenda above the love of God. It is a false counterfeit system that portrays a form of godliness but denies the power of God (2 Timothy 3:5). It stands as a barrier to those who hunger and thirst for righteousness

(righteousness, meaning "doing it God's way"), and denies access to the Spirit of freedom which is found in His presence (2 Corinthians 3:17).

In some ways the church of God has become a professional corporation. The kingdom of God and Christianity were never meant to be a corporation or professional entity. A Christian is a disciple and follower of Christ, meaning that as He is, so are we in this world. The problem then with professionalising the gospel or turning church into a company is that policies, rules and standards need to be upheld to maintain a good reputation.

However, my bible tells me that those who are born of the Spirit are unpredictable, you don't know which way they will turn. You can't systemise "true" Christianity. If He is our example then we should just examine one day in the life of Christ. You will notice devils manifesting, diseases healed, the uncompromised Word of God being preached to challenge people and bring them into the deeper things of the kingdom, all of which offended those in a corporation and professional type religion (aka the Pharisees).

Corporation and professional Christianity does not facilitate or accommodate the move of the Spirit of God, nor is it the wineskin that will give birth to the true sons of God the earth and creation are groaning for. The modern day corporate Christianity is just another face of religion that fulfils the agendas and purposes of man while sacrificing the manifest presence of God.

When the presence of God is manifest, anything can and will happen. Therefore, the wineskin of a corporate professional gospel gives no room for the "true" person of God (which is His presence) to manifest.

I don't think a life in the day of Jesus looked polished. In fact devils manifesting, people wanting to throw Him off a cliff, laying hands on lepers, spitting on dirt and rubbing the mud on someone's eyes, telling people they had to eat His flesh and drink His blood to enter the kingdom, doesn't look very corporate or professional to me.

It doesn't mean though, that there are no governing standards or order in the Kingdom of God, it just implies that when the Word of God is our standard and order there will be room and freedom for the Lord to manifest by His Spirit. Paul's epistles explain the governing order in the church through leadership. However, religion systemises things AWAY from the Word of God and His order. Yes, there must be accountability, leadership, true authority under the governance of the Word of God. But cultures and systems that hijack God's presence and prevent the Spirit from moving, keep God's people immature and hinder them from rising into true sonship. If church looked like how the Word of God explained it, there would be a rightful governance with maturity and purity which would develop followers who lay down their lives for Him and each other in the reverence of Christ. The Lord did not pay a price for His people to feed upon the plastic fantastic watered down self-serving gospel that religion promotes. He delivered the authentic unadulterated Word of God and preached it with signs and wonders following.

The story of King David bringing the ark of the covenant to Jerusalem (2 Samuel 6) is a great reminder that the power and authority of kingdom government cannot rest upon man-made traditions and structures.

The ark of the covenant housed the tablets of stone with the 10 commandments. David's intention was honourable, in fact he was a man after God's own heart and desired God's presence in Jerusalem, Israel's governmental headquarters. Unfortunately, he approached this task, lacking the fear of God.

The Lord had defined a specific protocol regarding the handling of the ark of the covenant. After examining Exodus 25:13-14 and Numbers 4:15; 7:9, the sons of Kohath were designated to carry the ark on their shoulders.

David chose, however, to ignore this instruction and placed the ark of the covenant on a wagon instead. As the story unfolds, the oxen pulling the wagon stumbled and Uzzah, one of David's men, was struck dead by God for stretching forth his hand to steady the ark. In those days, the ark of the covenant represented God's government and presence in Israel. David tried to restore the Lord's government via an inferior plan derived from his own mind, but clearly did not follow God's blueprint which brought forth severe consequences. His lack of reverence regarding the sacred articles (the government of God) kindled the Lord's displeasure, resulting in Uzzah's death. This is what happens when people operate in God's power and authority outside of His divine order. It is a prophetic picture of the governmental operation of God's divine order. The Lord's government cannot be built upon works of man (represented by the wagon). The systems and blueprints of man cannot house, nor are worthy of carrying God's glory, governmental power and authority.

Praise the Lord, David went away and reflected on his failed attempt to restore the ark of the covenant back in the centre of Israel's worship. When he returned a second time, he followed God's order in handling the ark of the covenant and removed his kingly robes in reverential fear and honour of God's presence. He worshipped before the presence of the Lord with all his might and without restrictions. By wearing a linen ephod, David lost sight of his own importance and need to be seen. The linen ephod hindered sweat and is what priests wore those days who ministered in the temple. It signifies ministering unto the Lord without earthy efforts (represented by sweat), or in other words not by might, nor by power, but *by His Spirit*. David was prophetically proclaiming the position anyone in authority should take in God's presence. However, he was scorned by his wife Michal (King Saul's daughter). David responded to her mocking insults by declaring that he would lower himself even further. His display of humility was the correct position to take in God's order of the fear of the Lord. The Lord said He would establish Messiah's rule upon the throne of David, who had a heart after God, and understood humility and reverence, enabling him to govern in the kingdom.

Beware Of The Leaven Of The Pharisees

In Matthew 16:6, Jesus warned His disciples to beware of the leaven of the Pharisees. It is widely understood that the Pharisees represent the spirit of religion, promoting man-made structures void of God's heart. These are systems built in the "name of God", but not led by the Spirit of God. Religion is geared towards giving glory to man, whereas being Spirit-led will always glorify God.

1 Corinthians 3:11-13

> *For no other foundation can anyone lay than that which is [already] laid, which is Jesus Christ (the Messiah, the Anointed One). But if anyone builds upon the Foundation, whether it be with gold, silver, precious stones, wood, hay, straw, The work of each [one] will become [plainly, openly] known (shown for what it is); for the day [of Christ] will disclose and declare it, because it will be revealed with fire, and the fire will test and critically appraise the character and worth of the work each person has done.*

This passage of scripture shows that it is possible to build upon the foundation of Jesus Christ with wood, hay and straw, representing man's works and efforts apart from the leading of the Holy Spirit. As seen in Genesis 11 with the building of the great tower of Babel, man is capable of building grandeur, magnificent establishments. However, if that man-made kingdom and establishment is built in the "name of God", upon the foundation of Jesus Christ, it must go through the test of fire to verify if it was in fact birthed of God (led by His Spirit).

Religious structures, representing a "form of godliness" without God's power, are constructed to promote man's skills, reputations and strength. This is the leaven of the Pharisees which Jesus warned about. Leaven also known as yeast is the raising agent used in bread, symbolising the pride of man. If the Pharisees represent religious systems of man and leaven refers to pride, then Jesus was warning His beloved to beware of religion as the root of it is pride.[69]

Jesus was not just warning them of the rules and traditions that religion promotes. He named the very aspect of religion that one must be on guard of and that is pride. Pride causes people to be yoked to their own strength, therefore, disqualifying them of governing in power and authority of the kingdom.

In this hour, God is shaking man-made foundations built on sand and He is re-establishing His people on firm foundations aligned with the Word of God.

Matthew 7:24-26

> *So everyone who hears these words of Mine and acts upon them [obeying them] will be like a sensible (prudent, practical, wise) man who built his house upon the rock. And the rain fell and the floods came and the winds blew and beat against that house; yet it did not fall, because it had been founded on the rock. And everyone who hears these words of Mine and does not do them will be like a stupid (foolish) man who built his house upon the sand.*

The rock represents the infallible, unshakable, tested Word of God. Throughout the two thousand years since the early church, the display of governmental authority through His people has been minimal. As noted in Hosea 6:2 the church now finds itself in need of reviving in order to walk in governmental capacity. This is due to the fact that many in the body of Christ have not heeded Jesus' warning, but instead have partaken of the leaven, exalting man's ideals above the Word of God. They have traded the keys of the kingdom (their right of sonship) for religion and Christianity based on

---

69   Darrell L. Bock, Mitch Glaser, "The meaning of Leaven in the Passover Seder", chosenpeople.com, accessed 01/29/2020, https://www.chosenpeople.com/site/the-meaning-of-leaven-in-the-passover-seder/

their own strength. Consequently, forfeiting their status as sons to the inferior position of orphans.

Orphans do not know their identity, they desire to know who they are and where they came from. Sons, on the other hand, know their Father and their inherited birthright. For this reason it is imperative to discover one's birthright and the foundations of how to govern "*by His Spirit, in His likeness*".

The Temptation To Prove Yourself

The Pharisees continually tried to trap Jesus into proving Himself by some sign or miracle. And so it is today, the enemy would seek to tempt you to PROVE yourself. In two out of the three temptations the devil incited Jesus to PROVE Himself while He was fasting in the wilderness.

Matthew 4:3

> *And the tempter came and said to Him, IF YOU ARE GOD'S SON, command these stones to be made [loaves of] bread.* (emphasis mine)

In other words, *prove* yourself. Some teachings have focused on the fact that Jesus was hungry and that the temptation was concerning food. I beg to differ and see the temptation directed at Jesus' security in His identity as a son.

In verse 4 (NKJV) Jesus' reply was simply obedience to the Word of God.

> *"It is written, man shall not live by bread alone, but by every word that proceeds out of the mouth of God."*

The devil again tempts Him to *prove* Himself in verse 5-6,

> *Then the devil took Him into the holy city and placed Him on a turret (pinnacle, gable) of the temple sanctuary. And he said to Him, IF YOU ARE THE SON OF GOD, throw Yourself down; for it is written, He will give His angels charge over you, and they will bear you up on their hands, lest you strike your foot against a stone. (emphasis mine)*

Again in verse 7 Jesus' response was the Word.

> *Jesus said to him, On the other hand, it is written also, You shall not tempt, test thoroughly, or try exceedingly the Lord your God.*

The third and final temptation:

Verse 8-9

> *Again, the devil took Him up on a very high mountain and showed Him all the kingdoms of the world and the glory (the splendor, magnificence, preeminence, and excellence) of them. And he said to Him, These things, all taken together, I will give You, if You will prostrate Yourself before me and do homage and worship me.*

Jesus' answer in verse 10:

> *Then Jesus said to him, Begone, Satan! For it has been written, You shall worship the Lord your God, and Him alone shall you serve.*

If the devil can succeed at tempting you to *prove* yourself, then He will have you surrender to the third temptation and have you WORSHIPPING him. The reason being that by proving yourself, you compromise obedience and forsake a spirit-led life for a flesh-driven life with striving performance. You are then no longer under Jesus' yoke which is light, but you have re-yoked yourself to the bond of slavery.

Jesus overcame not just by knowledge of the Word, but also by obedience and surrender to the Word. If He didn't know the Word, how then could He obey and overcome?

Folks the devil is after your worship, his ploy is and has always been to dumb the church down from walking by faith to walking by performance led rituals, self-serving systems and programs.

A hidden truth is that performance is idolatry as it seeks the adoration of another other than Abba.

Those who resist the temptation to perform, are ones who are fed and sustained by the meat of doing the will of their Father. They know too well their life source is not found in the opinions, criticisms, recognition and praises of mere men. They are secure in the affirmation of heavenly Father and KNOW for sure that they are sons.

Those who yield to the temptation to perform, don't really know who they are. Their inheritance of sonship hasn't been solidified because they still seek acceptance from this earthly realm to validate their heavenly gifts.

Saints, I hear an exhortation from Father. "My sons don't need to PROVE themselves, they just need to POSITION themselves."

Position yourself in the Word of God, let it be the anchor of your soul and the final verdict in your life. If you don't know the word of God for a situation you are facing right now, then seek it out, the answer will surely be there for you. The Lord once said to me "Don't freak out, find out!" Don't be deceived and yield to the temptation to perform and prove yourself, then wind up finding you are worshipping another in the process.

Don't bow the knee to this deception. Abba's love is sufficient. Position your heart in trust and use the word of God to put the devil in his place.

The Enemy Pride

The enemy tries to deceive mankind to be self-focused because he knows that when that happens the kingdom and glory of God cannot manifest. This has been a significant choke hold on the church.

Proverbs 18:12 (KJV)

> *Before destruction the heart of man is haughty, And before honor is humility.*

The word *honor* according to Strong's Concordance translates as: glory, weight, splendour.[70]

'Honor' is used throughout scripture, referring to glory and has the connotation of the Lord's glory displayed through His power and presence.

Before glory comes humility. Thus, the latter is clearly the position one must take to operate in the weight of God's glory. The enemy is also aware of this and deceives mankind to become self-centred, which hinders love between neighbours and disqualifies man from overcoming and governing in realms of authority.

The devil knows that where unity is, God commands a blessing. So he has sought to hijack the church of their authority and power by deceiving them to be self-absorbed.

---

70   James Strong. Strong's Expanded Exhaustive Concordance of the Bible (Nashville: Thomas Nelson, 2009), s.v *"honor"*

Proverbs 13:10 (NKJV)

> *By pride comes nothing but strife, But with the well-advised*
> *is wisdom.*

The word *well-advised* signifies to be teachable, which shows humility. However, pride separates, causes division, quarrels and arguments. Paul addresses this with the Corinthian church in 1 Corinthians 3:1-4. Firstly, he tells them he could not speak to them as mature believers but as mere infants, because of the state of their carnality. He explains why they are still infants or babes and exposes their conduct by stating that as long as envying, jealousy, wranglings and factions persist, they remain as unchanged men behaving according to human standards. Notice the issues that Paul addressed all revolved around strife, competition and division. The carnal realm points to pride, which denies Christians access to the *by His Spirit realm*, therefore preventing growth into sonship. For the spiritual person, humility is key and is the mark of the spiritually mature as opposed to knowledge. Many have relied on knowledge but have fallen short in regards to humility.

1 Corinthians 8:1

> *NOW ABOUT food offered to idols: of course we know that all*
> *of us possess knowledge [concerning these matters. Yet mere]*
> ***knowledge causes people to be puffed up*** *(to bear themselves*
> *loftily and be proud),* ***but love*** *(affection and goodwill and*
> *benevolence) edifies and* ***builds up and encourages one to***
> ***grow [to his full stature].*** *(emphasis mine)*

Mere knowledge does not qualify man to govern in the realm of kingdom authority. Paul the apostle was an expert in the Law of God and knew the Torah from back to front. Yet, he had to be humbled in his own sight, in the presence of Jesus, so God could position him in the seat of the kingdom he would possess (Acts 9).

Obadiah 1:3a

The pride of your heart has deceived you

Pride causes a person to be open to deception. However, those who take a humble position are receptive to the Lord's counsel and are able to admit when they are wrong.

1 Corinthians 13 reveals that denying oneself is imperative to walking in love. Without humility people cannot deny themselves, because pride will always seek its own desires and interests. When people put themselves and their own needs first, unity is forsaken.

Job 41 speaks about the Leviathan principality, which is described as the monarch over all the sons of pride (Job 41:24). In Isaiah 27:1, Isaiah prophesies the day that the Lord will deal with Leviathan, the swiftly, fleeing, twisting and winding serpent. This serpent creature is also known as the lying deceiver that tricked Eve in the garden, which resulted in a broken covenant relationship and separation from God. The lying, twisting principality continues its evil mandate, sowing lies amongst believers and seeking to divide and conquer. Those positioned in humility are protected from this evil. However, Christians, not fully crucified with Christ and with thrones of pride in their lives, would easily become prey to this evil spirit.

Jesus warned the people in Matthew 7:1-5 not to judge others, as this is not their governmental position. The judgement seat belongs to God and Him alone.

> *DO NOT judge and criticize and condemn others, so that you may not be judged and criticized and condemned yourselves. For just as you judge and criticize and condemn others, you will be judged and criticized and condemned, and in accordance with the measure you [use to] deal out to others, it will be dealt out again to you. Why do you stare from*

> *without at the very small particle that is in your brother's eye*
> *but do not become aware of and consider the beam of timber*
> *that is in your own eye? Or how can you say to your brother,*
> *Let me get the tiny particle out of your eye, when there is the*
> *beam of timber in your own eye? You hypocrite, first get the*
> *beam of timber out of your own eye, and then you will see*
> *clearly to take the tiny particle out of your brother's eye.*

Accusations and judgements are rooted in pride. Judgement will cause a person's perceptions on others and the situation to be distorted. If people do not judge themselves first, how could they help others in their shortcomings? They are unable to see clearly, and according to this scripture will bind themselves to the very shortcoming they were criticising others about. In other words, people's judgement of someone else's sin will cause them to stumble in that same sin themselves. They will find themselves transgressing in sins they would not normally be vulnerable to, if they had not first judged others in those sins (Romans 2:1-3).

Taking the seat of judgement without first assessing our own hearts is arrogance and the Lord calls it hypocritical. Judging a person's sin is not ruling, nor governing in the kingdom.

James 4:6 (NKJV)

> *But He gives us more grace. Therefore, He says: "God resists*
> *the proud, But gives grace to the humble."*

God resists the proud, because pride in the heart will position someone in direct competition with God for His glory. Satan is a prime example of this, he wanted the praise, honour and esteem of heaven and coveted God's glory, desiring it for himself. For this reason, we must never take the credit or boast about the good works Jesus has done through us. We should always check our heart motives for sharing these things with others. Is it to draw attention to ourselves or the Lord?

God's grace is His ability given to man via the Holy Spirit, it is His empowerment to overcome. God opposes those who refuse to yield to His authority and ways. But, to those who yield and surrender to His will, He gives more power. Humility is clearly the position of one who governs in the kingdom realm.

Submission To Authority Accesses Kingdom Authority

1 Peter 5:6

> *Therefore humble yourselves [demote, lower yourselves in your own estimation] under the mighty hand of God, that in due time He may exalt you,*

God's hand symbolises His authority. He will position His people in each season as they faithfully submit to His authority. The word exalt in this scripture does not refer to being puffed up and praised, but simply means God will position according to the times and seasons. Under the hand of God, is the place of submission to His authority and ability to perform on His saints' behalf. Throughout scripture, The Lord miraculously performed for His people by His mighty hand, with His hand signifying His power to move on people's behalf (Deuteronomy 26:8). This is when we as believers stop striving in our own efforts and are protected by being under His authority.

John Bevere writes in "Undercover", that Adam and Eve were protected while they remained under God's authority through obedience. The moment they sinned and rebelled against God they were no longer "covered".[71]

1 Peter 5:6 clearly stresses the importance of abiding under His mighty hand, namely that it enables believers to operate in the power and authority of the kingdom. If His people, however, do not submit and humble themselves under His authority, they step out of His protection and empowerment by His Spirit.

---

71   John Bevere, Undercover, 2

Proverbs 11:14

> *Where no wise guidance is, the people fall, but in the multitude*
> *of counselors there is safety.*

Remaining under God's authority is also being under man's authority. The Bible says to submit to one another as in the reverence of Christ (Ephesians 5:21). When pride is in people's hearts they will not want to be accountable to any kind of authority, they will isolate themselves and claim to only listen to Jesus. However, Proverbs 11:14, clearly states that there is safety when people surround themselves with a multitude of counsellors. As a minister, I have seen many leaders and Christians fall into sin because they refused to be accountable and rejected Godly counsel. Unfortunately, pride goes before destruction and haughtiness before a fall (Proverbs 16:18). A person who avoids accountability is a mere infant in Christ, filled with carnal rebellion and soulish desires. They cannot be trusted with governmental responsibility and power, as they reject sonship through pride.

Children in Christ are still filled with their own ways, but as they grow into maturity, being under God's hand becomes more desirable than living for themselves. The soul is disciplined when disobedience is punished by obedience, enabling the spirit man to rule over the flesh (2 Corinthians 10:6), which is called maturity or sonship. The soul is submitted to the authority of God and the spirit man is able to operate in the free realm of faith, by obedience to the leading of the Holy Spirit, as union with Him is established to the point of John 14:12-15 becoming reality.

> *I assure you, most solemnly I tell you, if anyone steadfastly*
> *believes in Me, he will himself be able to do the things that I*
> *do; and he will do even greater things than these, because I*
> *go to the Father. And I will do [I Myself will grant] whatever*
> *you ask in My Name [as presenting all that I AM], so that the*
> *Father may be glorified and extolled in (through) the Son.*
> *[Yes] I will grant [I Myself will do for you] whatever you*

shall ask in My Name [as presenting all that I Am]. If you [really] love Me, you will keep (obey) My commands.

Paul exhorted the church to remain within their God-given jurisdiction in order to successfully operate in their governmental capacity. In the body of Christ, like in any army, there is rank and file and it takes humility to walk within each one's jurisdiction in governmental authority.

Romans 12:3 (NKJV)

For I say, through the grace given to me, to everyone who is among you, not to think of himself more highly than he ought to think, but to think soberly, as God has dealt to each one a measure of faith.

A Christian's measure of faith is their advanced information given to them by God and it is their jurisdiction of authority. This is what Jesus meant by not doing anything outside of what He saw His Father do. He was only walking in obedience to the leading of God, which is how He remained in authority. Too many times, however, believers try to operate outside of their jurisdiction. If this weren't true, Paul would not have addressed the church in this manner. His exhortation was to highlight the fact that they were operating in pride. They were thinking of themselves more highly than they ought and in the following verses he explains that these people do not function successfully in the part of the body assigned to them. When believers operate outside of jurisdiction, they become isolated, are unable to function as team players and the whole body is compromised and disjointed. Examples of this are pastors trying to be prophets, evangelists attempting to be teachers or even those flowing in a governmental capacity of the five-fold ministry, who are called but not yet appointed by God. Many believers are enlightened to their calling of what the Lord would seek to do in and through their lives, but fail to humble themselves under His hand so He can train and mature them into that capacity. They try to operate out of season, and think of themselves more important than they ought. They may understand they have a prophetic calling, but step outside jurisdiction, assuming they can correct mature leaders and the body of Christ without any development of submission to authority in their lives. To function in authority as believers, submission to God's and man's authority is fundamentally vital.

Hidden In Christ – The Seat Of Ruling And Reigning

Matthew 6:1

> *TAKE CARE not to do your good deeds publicly or before men, **in order** to be seen by them; otherwise you will have no reward [reserved for and awaiting you] with and from your Father Who is in heaven. (emphasis mine)*

Here the Lord is not saying not to do any deeds publicly, but is highlighting the motive of the heart to be seen or gain recognition. Jesus often did good deeds publicly, He healed the sick, delivered the captives, taught the multitudes, but never to give glory to Himself but to God.

This scripture exhorts God's people to maintain a pure heart. The Lord reveals that there are rewards for good deeds, acts of faith done in obedience to His Word. However, these rewards are only available if the good deeds were done with pure motives.

The passage of scripture continues,

Verse 2

> *Thus, whenever you give to the poor, do not blow a trumpet before you, as the hypocrites in the synagogues and in the streets like to do, **that they may be recognized and honored** and **praised by men**. Truly I tell you, they have their reward in full already. (emphasis mine)*

What is the reward for those who desire to be seen? It is the praises of men. That is what they sought, and that is why they did what they did. It was all from a wrong heart motive.

Jesus is inviting His people to operate from a *higher* level of kingdom authority. When God's people do good deeds from a pure heart motive, they are able to affect the eternal realm and operate above the dictates of man's approval or disapproval. The rewards of the Lord are received from the eternal realm, therefore those who seek their reward from this earthly realm are limited to operate within this realm. As long as man's approval and recognition is obtained, the deed would be validated. However, there are scriptural examples of good deeds Jesus did that were not seen as favourable and honourable in His culture. One example where Jesus' good deeds were challenged is in Mark 3:1-6. The Pharisees challenged Jesus regarding healing a man on the Sabbath because it went against their interpretation of God's Law. They were exalting culture above liberty. In fact, they were so angered by this good deed that did not line up with culture, they sought to kill Him.

Another example that can be explored in modern culture is the liberty to give Godly counsel to homosexuals or transgenders. Different governments around the world are seeking to pass laws that restrict or forbid ministers and medical professionals from advising and counselling homosexuals and transgenders to change their orientation.

People who seek glory in their good deeds are bound by the natural rules of man's opinions and approval, hindering them from operating in the fullness of kingdom authority. If they only do good deeds for praise and recognition, without the motive of liberating captives, then they have abandoned their governmental birthright of being Spirit-led. The Spirit of God does not bow to the laws and traditions of man, on the contrary, His ways are higher and those who follow Him, must operate from a higher position. Ironically, this elevated place above the world's ways is obtaining a "lower" position on the earth, namely humility.

Luke 10:19- 20

> *Behold! I have given you authority and power to trample upon*
> *serpents and scorpions, and [physical and mental strength*
> *and ability] over all the power that the enemy [possesses];*
> *and nothing shall in any way harm you. Nevertheless, do not*
> *rejoice at this, that the spirits are subject to you, but rejoice*
> *that your names are enrolled in heaven.*

Jesus was led by the Spirit of God in every deed He did. There are countless examples of the different ways He operated in healing and deliverance. Sometimes He spat on dirt and used the mud to heal blindness (John 9:6), other times He just spoke the word without touching the person and they were healed (Luke 7:1-10).

Each time He ministered, He was led by His Father and in full surrender to His authority. If He was moved by the praises or disapproval of man, His judgement would have been clouded and the kingdom would not have flowed through Him. He would not have been able to discern what to do in the moment, under the pressure of crowds watching. Interestingly, He not only performed miracles in front of people, but also away from the crowd.

Those whose purpose is to let the Saviour of the kingdom flow through them, are willing to lay down their lives, but performers, on the other hand, seek glory for themselves. Think about it, a performer is first of all motivated to entertain and in response receive the applause of man. In a platform of performance, the person submits to the authority of man's formulas. Formats and procedures are followed to preserve reputation and maintain man's approval.

Kingdom thrives in an environment of authenticity and humility as opposed to religion which cannot survive under these conditions. These two fundamental keys of the kingdom (authenticity and humility) are born from true identity in sonship. Humility is knowing who you are, because when you know who you are, you know who you are *without* Him. Authenticity originates from identity, whereas copycats have no idea who they are.

If Jesus was motivated by honour and glory, He would have been a performer and not a saviour. To be a saviour, He laid down His life.

Colossians 3:3-4

> *For [as far as this world is concerned] you have died, and your [new real] life is **hidden** with Christ in God. When Christ, who is our life, appears, then you also will appear with Him in [the splendor of His] glory. (emphasis mine)*

When believers receive Christ, they die to the world and the dictates of it. They are now *in* Christ, Who is to be glorified through them. God's people are able to carry heaven's authority *through* Christ, by being *hidden* in Him. Isaiah 9:6 says the government of God has been put upon Messiah's shoulders, meaning only HE is able to carry heaven's power and authority upon His shoulders, because He paid the ultimate price. It is impossible to carry heaven's authority and power *separate* from Christ, nor operate in it in mere human strength, wisdom, efforts or means. When you are hidden in Christ, and are operating from Him (being like Jesus and only doing what they see their Father do, John 5:19), then you are truly walking in governmental authority.

You cannot create separate from the Holy Spirit's leading and expect heaven's endorsement of power and authority to be upon it. Anything created or done outside of the Holy Spirit's leading is not birthed of God and is carnal. It may be a "good" thing, but it is not a "God" thing. Good things do not overcome the world, only God things do. "Good" things usually hold an earthly agenda for the glorification of man. "God" things always maintain a heavenly agenda for the glorification of God and for the benefit of man.

To be hidden in Christ means that Jesus is glorified in the believer's life, because that person is operating by His leading from a place of surrender.

The Mantle Of Humility –
The Highest Rank In The Kingdom

Walking in kingdom authority is different from operating in a gift of the spirit. The gifts and callings of God are irrevocable (Romans 11:29), that's why sinners and backslidden Christians can operate in a gifting and power, but Jesus will say to them at the end of the age, "Depart from Me for I never knew you." (Matthew 7:21-23) Shifting demonic governmental structures and realms is different from operating in a gift and is reserved for those who are dead to this world and are hidden in Christ. Kingdom authority carries the breaker anointing and through the obedience and surrender of the believer walking in union with Christ, the earth will witness things being broken open, demonic rulership displaced and Godly order established. Territories will be taken, victory will be secured, as the apostolic third day church moves from the hidden place in Christ, and begins to comprehend the formula for kingdom authority. No longer seeking to make a name for themselves, but instead making Jesus famous throughout all the earth.

John 12:32 (KJV)

> *And I, if I be lifted up from the earth, will draw all men unto me.*

The mandate of God's people is to lift His name high, not the name of a ministry, title, organization, or their good deeds. When His people align with this understanding, the great commission can be accomplished and mankind will be drawn unto Jesus. For too long the people of God have sought to make a name for themselves and have exalted establishments and movements in the "name of Christ" with the wrong heart motive and agenda. John the Baptist declared in John 3:30 that he must decrease and Jesus increase, because he understood the principles of the kingdom. Along with preparing the hearts of the people to receive Messiah, his commission was also to *reveal* and *unveil* the lamb of God to the world. This assignment has not ceased, because when believers take this position of humility (proclaiming that they decrease, so He might increase), the Lord will be revealed to a hurting, dying, dark and lost world. True governmental authority rests on those who are hidden in Christ and seek no desire for notoriety or fame.

Rick Joyner, in his book "The Final Quest", describes an encounter he had with the mantle of humility. He had gone to the heights of the third heaven and from there had gained a rank of great value. His armor shone bright and brilliant, pleasant to the eye of those who beheld him. An angel that was accompanying him on the journey of this heavenly encounter handed him a garment to put on, which was shabby-looking and ugly to the eye. The angel explained that he would not be able to see without wearing this mantle. When he asked the angel why he had to put on the cloak, the angel informed him it was the mantle of humility. Rick, reluctantly put this mantle on. The angel expounded that it was the highest rank in the kingdom and that Jesus wore it as well on the earth. With this mantle on, no power in heaven or earth could stand against, and there was no greater position than being clothed in His grace. Only those who wore the mantle as well would be able to see and know Rick Joyner's rank.[72]

This encounter is filled with wise counsel. In the heart of man is a desire to be seen, recognised, praised and receive accolades. Those who are humble will recognise others of high rank among them, but those clouded by their own conceit will not, because they are carnal and interpret things from outward appearance, sense and reason. This in itself is a motivation to wear the cloak of humility, because then people with wrong motives and prideful, untrustworthy attitudes will be exposed to those wearing the mantle. Believers do not need to be seen, but to be truly secure and protected from deception, the cloak of humility is the greatest treasure one can possess.

---

72   Rick Joyner, "The Final Quest", 61,62,68

The Day I Learned It Takes Humility To Operate In Faith

Self-preservation is surely the enemy of those called to rule and reign. I recall a time early in my walk with the Lord where He began to show me what my purpose for being here on this earth was. He revealed that I was called into the five-fold ministry and He had a job for me to fulfil. By nature, I am a very shy person, I always have been, since I was a young child. I would not enjoy meeting new people and hide behind my mother's skirt. Speaking in front of people was my greatest fear. I feared failing, looking silly, not being perfect and getting it wrong. I was riddled with so much insecurity and self-centredness. So, when I felt the call of God to go to bible college and train for ministry, my flesh resisted wholeheartedly. I began to make excuses why I did not need to go in that direction and how maybe one day I would just fall into my calling. This is amusing now when I look back on it. The Lord, knowing I was struggling with fear of man and self-preservation, came to me in a dream. This dream changed the very course of my life, because He showed me how I was being governed by fear and that it would be the downfall of my life. When I woke up from the dream, He took me straight to Jeremiah 1:17,

> *But you [Jeremiah], gird up your loins! Arise and tell them*
> *all that I command you. Do not be dismayed and break down*
> *at the sight of their faces, lest I confound you before them and*
> *permit you to be overcome.*

I think this is the first time I really encountered the fear of God. As mentioned in the earlier chapter, the fear of the Lord will drive out the fear of man. I knew according to this scripture that if I chose to save my life I would never be an overcomer or do anything significant for God. Fear of man and self-preservation would cause me to live a life of failure and defeat. I had to choose to lay my life down, and that included my pride, insecurities, fear of failure and risk rejection, in order to obey God. It requires humility to walk

163

by faith, but it is by faith that you overcome the world, govern and are more than a conqueror.

Keys To Overcoming And The Power Of His Resurrection

Revelation 12:11 (KJV)

And they overcame him by the blood of the Lamb, and by the word of their testimony; and they loved not their lives unto the death.

Testimony is powerful. Being hidden in Christ does not mean that you cannot share testimonies. But the true testimony of Jesus is to declare the victory of Christ through the blood of the Lamb. We should not be testifying of ourselves. Many testify of how Christ is operating so powerfully through them, but they are not lifting up the testimony of Christ. They are testifying for the purpose of exalting themselves, how special and anointed they are that God is moving through them. They have received their reward, the praises of man.

Overcoming by the blood of the Lamb is making the statement that true victory is only found because of His sacrifice that deemed humanity access to freedom. Upon this truth is where we flow, move, decree and govern.

Loving not our lives even unto death is the third key to overcome according to this scripture. When God's people lose sight of self and declare it is no longer I who lives but Christ who lives within me, and are willing to pay the price for the gospel, there will be such a glorious display of kingdom power and authority on this earth. The believer can truly enter into the power of His resurrection from this place of death.

Resurrection power is only operative upon that which is dead. Something alive does not need to be made alive. Hence, resurrection power flows through believers who have surrendered their lives to Christ and have taken up their crosses to follow Him (Matthew 16:24-26).

Jesus makes it very clear that to follow Him, we must first count the cost... The price is nothing more than our lives.[73]

---

73   Bevere, the Fear of the lord. 55

Chapter 8:

GOVERNING IN THE JUSTICE OF GOD

The Meek Shall Inherit The Earth

Meekness is not usually a word you hear often when describing the overcoming, governmental power of God. However, it is a required virtue to partner with God in establishing His will, purposes and plans on the earth. As discussed earlier, governing with true authority, is submission under the Father.

Jesus said in John 5:19, *"The Son can do nothing of Himself, but what He sees the Father do."* In other words, *"I don't do anything unless I first see my Father do it."* Whatever situation believers find themselves in, they should take no action outside of what they hear or see from the Father. To accomplish this, great bridled strength and restraint is requisite, which is called *meekness*.

Mathew 5:5 (NKJV)

Blessed are the meek, For they shall inherit the earth.

God wants His people to inherit the earth. Psalm 2:8 encourages us to ask of the Lord that He would give us the nations as our inheritance and the earth as our possession. The Lord has given His people the earth to rule, govern and take dominion. Sons participate in God's inheritance, which is their possession. Thus, the Lord is saying in this verse, that He is going to share governmental authority, to rule and reign over the earth with the meek.

The definition of *meek* in Greek according to the Strong's concordance is: humble, mild, gentle.[74]

The definition of *meek* in the Thayer's Greek Lexicon dictionary states that meekness toward God is that disposition of spirit in which people accept His dealing with them as good, and therefore without disputing or resisting. In the Old Testament, the meek are those wholly relying on God rather than their own strength to defend against injustice. Gentleness or meekness is the opposite to self-assertiveness and self-interest. It stems from trust in God's goodness and control over the situation. The gentle person is not occupied with self at all. This is a work of the Holy Spirit, not of the human will.[75]

There is a vast difference between the earthly view of strength and God's. God's definition of strength is being bridled in humility, which is meekness. It is the opposite to pride, rebellion, complaining and whining. Meekness is to understand that God is the boss and submit first to His wisdom without disputing or resisting.

According to Thayer's explanation above, meek individuals are those who trust God to defend them rather than yield to anger, wrath and revenge. Meekness is not weakness, but the ability to rely on God for His justice to be demonstrated on your behalf, in the midst of opposition or injustice. It demands a great amount of restraint and strength as it is a fruit and a work of the Spirit.

---

74   James Strong. Strong's Expanded Exhaustive Concordance of the Bible
      (Nashville: Thomas Nelson, 2009), s.v *"meek"*
75   Joseph Thayer, *Thayer's Greek English Lexicon*, Hendrickson Publishers, 1995. *s.v. "meek"*

The Meekest Man On Earth Was
A Man Entrusted With Government

Numbers 12:3

> *Now the man Moses was very meek (gentle, kind, and humble)*
> *or above all the men on the face of the earth.*

Moses was the meekest man on the face of the earth and was chosen by God to lead his nation from slavery into freedom. He received and brought the Law of God (the Ten Commandments) to the people, representing a man of government.

Moses was entrusted by God with great responsibility, governmental authority and power. He used Moses to display His supernatural power before the people, by moving in great power, signs and wonders and yet Moses was the meekest man on earth! However, Moses was not always that way, in a time of awakening to his destiny, he struck and killed a slave master, while witnessing Pharaoh's unjust treatment towards his people, the Israelites (Exodus 2:11-15). He fled into the wilderness where he remained for 40 years before meeting the Lord at the burning bush. Moses yielded to the indignation that was ignited in his heart and took vengeance into his own hands. We must comprehend that anger in itself is not a sin, it is an emotion that God has given to man to realize when a boundary has been crossed. But the Lord instructs His people not to sin when infuriated (Ephesians 4:26). Meekness acts as a bridle to prevent sin in moments of anger.

Romans 12:19-21

> *Beloved, never avenge yourselves, but leave the way open*
> *for [God's] wrath; for it is written, Vengeance is Mine, I will*
> *repay (requite), says the Lord. But if your enemy is hungry,*
> *feed him; if he is thirsty, give him drink; for by doing so you*

will heap burning coals upon his head. Do not let yourself be overcome by evil, but overcome (master) evil with good.

When people take revenge into their own hands, they block God's righteous judgement, which is the best justice of all. His saints are not to let evil be their master by letting it overcome them, because evil will rule and dictate their emotions. They then say and do the wrong things, respond in evil, walk in the flesh and the fruit of the Spirit will not be able to operate in their lives. God's justice is perfect and His scales are evenly balanced. His people must instead make way for God's justice by overcoming evil with good.

Psalm 37:7-11

*Be still and rest in the Lord; wait for Him and patiently lean yourself upon Him; fret not yourself because of him who prospers in his way, because of the man who brings wicked devices to pass. Cease from anger and forsake wrath; **fret not yourself – it only tends to evil doing**. For evildoers shall be cut off, but those who wait and hope and look for the Lord shall inherit the earth. For yet a little while, and the evildoers will be no more; though you look with care where they used to be, they will not be found. But the meek shall inherit the earth and shall delight themselves in the abundance of peace. (emphasis mine)*

Acting in your own strength or wisdom does not make wrongs right, nor does it overthrow the principalities and powers at work in the production of evil on earth. If we freak out and take matters into our own hands, thinking that others are getting away with evil, we will end up transgressing ourselves. This will then disqualify us from operating in governmental authority in that situation until we repent and do it God's way. People who know how to connect with the counsel and wisdom of God through the reverential fear of the Lord will be able to defeat evil on a spiritual level, which will then manifest in justice and a turnaround on the earth. Moses' act of anger was futile and did not liberate His people, instead it caused another forty year delay before Moses was ready for the job.

Delivering God's Justice God's Way

After spending forty years in the wilderness, the Lord sent him to deliver His people Israel from the bondage of slavery in Egypt. Moses did not have a plan to attack or avenge, but he yielded to God's instruction and blueprint of justice to rescue the Israelites. Although, Moses needed boldness to confront Pharaoh, meekness was the underlying bridle enabling God to entrust him with power and authority. Meekness was a prerequisite for delivering God's justice His way. Moses was patient with the outworking of the ten plagues. He did not complain or tell God that another strategy would be better, but remained meek, mild and gentle.

Another example of the display of God's justice is in Numbers 12. Miriam and Aaron (Moses' own brother and sister) were speaking against him because he married a wife from another nation, not of their colour or people, which displeased them. Scripture says that God heard their conversation and came down in the pillar of a cloud in the tent of meeting to rebuke Aaron and Miriam. The Lord told them that He speaks to Moses face to face and that he is more than a prophet. When the cloud lifted, Miriam became leprous. Aaron then begged Moses to ask God for mercy on Miriam's behalf, which he did, but God said she had to stay outside the camp for seven days until she was cured and could return. This is a clear depiction of Moses not having to defend himself and the Lord rebuking and chastising those who unjustly accused him.

Meekness Is The Answer To Justice

Moses did not defend himself to Aaron and Miriam by saying, "Do you not know that I am the chosen one? If not for me, you would have still been stuck in Egypt." No, Moses did not say that, because he was humble and mild of manner. This pleased God and He, therefore, spoke in Moses' defence.

Meekness will not only cause you to wait for God's vengeance, but also His promotion.

David understood this principle as he was being pursued by King Saul, who was unjustly trying to kill him. David had only done good to Saul, by risking his life to slay Goliath, fighting on the front lines in war and by playing the harp to calm Saul who was tormented by evil spirits. Unfortunately, Saul was jealous and repaid David's good with evil. David, therefore, became a vagabond, running for his life, living in caves like a wild man stripped of all comforts and security, and for doing absolutely nothing wrong. It was complete injustice and David paid a high price for Saul's insecurities.

In 1 Samuel 24 David gained a prime opportunity to take vengeance into his own hands and he could have even justified it. When Saul entered the cave (where David was hiding) to find privacy and relief, David's own men suggested that the Lord had delivered his enemy into his hands. Saul was in a vulnerable position, unaware and unable to defend himself and could have easily been sprung upon. But, David would have had to transgress in order to avenge and he knew that this was not of God. If one must transgress God's Word to gain advantage, it certainly is not the Lord's leading. David was aware that he had to wait for God's justice and promotion.

It would have been easy or tempting for David to think that God had brought him this opportunity, as he was next in line to be king. He could have thought, I can end this madness now and return to my homeland, and I will no longer have to live like a vagabond running for my life, because this very enemy that caused me all this grief is at my mercy. But, it was through meekness that David restrained from touching God's anointed, promoting himself before his time and from using his own power to bring justice. Instead, he allowed God to bring justice in His timing and David was promoted in the right season.

Because David was a man submitted under the authority of God in the fear of the Lord, he was able to see clearly in a situation that would otherwise have been confusing. Those who are not submitted under His authority are a law unto themselves and are open to deception, easily interpreting a scenario of treason as lawful.

David was tested whether he would take vengeance on Saul, but obviously his meekness enabled him to trust God to fight his battles. Meekness is therefore a vital key in governing and using authority the right way.

Meekness – The Governmental Yoke Of His Rest

In Numbers 20, Moses stepped out of meekness and used his authority in disobedience, costing him the privilege of entering the promised land.

Miriam had passed away and the Israelites were complaining to Moses that there was no water. Moses sought the Lord for counsel and He told Moses to speak to the rock. But, Moses struck the rock with his staff instead, releasing his built up frustrations regarding the Israelites, whom he addressed as a rebellious people. The Lord was greatly displeased with this act of disobedience, because he stepped out of meekness and surrender to God's authority, and yielded to anger. The water still flowed, but it was not under God's obedience. Moses was therefore disqualified from entering the promised land, which is a prophetic symbol of the "rest".

Meekness is being able to carry the yoke of God and walk in the rest.

Matthew 11:29

> *Take My yoke upon you and learn from Me, for I am **gentle (meek)** and **humble (lowly)** in heart, and you will find rest (relief and ease and refreshment and recreation and blessed quiet) for your souls. (emphasis mine)*

To walk in the rest (by His Spirit) one must take on the yoke of God, which is humble and gentle (meekness). The Lord is meek, not harsh or hard pressing. His yoke is the rest of God, trusting Him and His way in all things and operating by His Spirit. This is where rest for the soul is found. Outside of the rest, we walk around vexed, striving in our own efforts, anxious and stirred up with offence and anger that leads to bitterness. Those who fail to submit to His way are not able to enter the rest. Therefore, the Lord tells us to take on Jesus's yoke of meekness, to trust Him for justice and yield to His way, which leads to rest and relief for our souls.

Meekness – Power That Releases Justice

Meekness is NOT passivity. Jesus was not passive, but totally yielded to His Father's authority, and He understood the authority of heaven available to Him. When Jesus was crucified, He could have called upon a legion of angels to justify Himself in the midst of this injustice He was enduring for humanity. But because of His meekness, He fully obeyed God and did not get off the cross. Jesus' crucifixion was the greatest injustice the world has ever seen, but simultaneously also the greatest justice, because those who accept His sacrifice become sons of God. God's justice is different to man's. God's justice saw fit for Jesus, a perfect man, to take on humanity's sins, in order to make us righteous and 'justified'. Thanks to His meekness, He could restrain from calling down a legion of angels to rescue Him, consequently making way for the true justice of God to deliver mankind from the law of sin and death! This powerful display of meekness saved humanity from death and hell. Thus, meekness is absolutely not weakness, but reigned power causing the justice of God to be released.

Meekness is essential in order to rule and reign effectively. His people need to demonstrate the Lord's power under His authority in order to establish lasting results of true restitution and justice. It is time for principalities, powers and rulers of darkness to surrender to the government of God on this earth. Let the meek inherit the earth.

Chapter 9:

GOVERNANCE –
THE REWARD OF THE FAITHFUL

Servants Or Sons?

At times there can be confusion around the words *servant* and *son*. Some think we are no longer servants and misinterpret this role as a slave. True, we are no longer slaves, we are children of God, and being a servant of the Lord is very different from being a slave. There are three progressions in the kingdom. When we are born again we become *children* of God (Romans 8:15-16). Then as we mature we are promoted to *servants* of God (Luke 12:42-44). Numerous scriptures portray *serving* in the kingdom as a promotion and a privilege (Matthew 25:23). Finally, when we have been proven faithful in the role of servants and our faith and faithfulness have been tested and tried, we are promoted into *sonship*. Sonship is the highest rank in the kingdom and it is when we govern.

To put it simply, we are sons who *serve* in our Father's kingdom. Many of Jesus' parables surround the notion of servanthood and stewardship of the kingdom of God. As a son/daughter of God I *serve* His purposes here on earth. As a minister I *serve* His people and I minister (*serve*) unto the Lord.

However, this servitude comes from the position of sonship, knowing that He has granted me all His authority to act on His behalf as He "leads" me *by His Spirit.*

If you have a family business, a restaurant for example, your aim might be to pass the family business down to your children as an inheritance. When your children are born they are too young for any kind of responsibility. Pretty much everything is done for them as they are taught how to do things for themselves. Little by little they start learning responsibility and are given more as they prove faithful with each stage of development. They are then promoted to *serve* in the restaurant. In order to run the family business they will first need to "work" in the family business to apprehend responsibility and 'manage' staff, expenses, income etc. and gain success with the "inheritance" until it is finally handed over. It would be foolish to hand over the inheritance to someone without knowledge and experience in the business or who does not appreciate the hard work involved in running it. If I owned a restaurant and I was planning to hand it over to my son, I would not allow him to sit at the table with his feet up eating and dining, enjoying all the privileges of what I have worked for. He would have to work and appreciate the privilege of ownership (which is what sonship is), his inheritance. Furthermore, he would have to be proven responsible with making decisions and stewarding the business I have built, which is called servanthood. This is comparable to God's house. We serve faithfully in His house before we are promoted to our governmental seat of ruling and reigning.

Characteristics Of The Faithful

Strong's Concordance translates the word *faithful* from the Greek, meaning: trustworthy, believing, sure, true.

It comes from the root Greek word *Peitho*, which signifies: to convince, to agree, to assure, believe and have confidence, persuade, trust and yield.[76]

---

[76]   James Strong. Strong's Expanded Exhaustive Concordance of the Bible
        (Nashville: Thomas Nelson, 2009), s.v *"faithful"*

Wow! It is interesting that one of the translations of faithful is *believing*. A faithful person in essence is a person of faith, and faithfulness is a fruit of faith. We are reminded in Hebrews 3 that the children of Israel who were in unbelief were unable to enter and possess the promised land, which was their promised inheritance. Unbelief, therefore, shows God that He cannot trust us with the inheritance. The Israelites were not fully *persuaded* (another meaning Strong's has used in the Greek translation of the word *faithful*), or did not trust God's character that He would do what He said He would do. God took this as a personal insult and the unbelieving attitude of the people caused unfaithfulness.

Other words used to describe the word *faithful* in various dictionaries are: constant, loyal, stable, dependable, long continued steadfastness, steadfastness to whatever one is bound to by a pledge. That is why God tests our faith. He tests our pledge of allegiance to Him and whether or not we believe what He says. If we believe His Word and are fully persuaded, it displays trustworthiness, stability and reliability regardless of whether the circumstances are favourable or not. It also denotes that you are established, because when you believe and have confidence in Him, you can build and support the kingdom however He leads you.

James 1:3

> *Be assured and understand that the trial and proving of your faith bring out endurance and* **steadfastness** *and patience. (emphasis mine)*

This suggests that the Lord will test your faith (what you believe) to produce faithfulness in you. Another word for faithfulness is steadfastness which is important to the Lord as a servant and minister unto His people. God can depend, rely and trust a faithful, trustworthy person who has been tested and tried and has not walked away from Him; these are the ones He will promote.

I guess after studying the meaning of faithfulness we can understand why the Lord said in Proverbs 20:6 *"Who can find a faithful man?"* It is a rare and precious attribute.

Nehemiah 9:7-8

> *You are the Lord, the God Who chose Abram and brought him out of Ur of the Chaldees and gave him the name Abraham.* **You found his heart faithful before You, and You made covenant with him to** *give his descendants the land of the Canaanite, Hittite, Amorite, Perizzite, Jebusite, and Girgashite. And You have fulfilled Your promise, for You are just and righteous. (emphasis mine)*

Abraham *believed* God and it was accounted to him as righteousness. He was faithful because he believed and the Lord was not looking for just anyone, but for a faithful person to enter into covenant with.

Think about it, someone who is persuaded in who God is and believes His Word, is reliable, true, sure, trustworthy, unshakeable and able to be trusted with representing Him in a position of authority.

Faithfulness – A Requirement Of Governance

A faithful person does what is in the Lord's heart and mind.

1 Samuel 2:35

> *And I will raise up for Myself a faithful priest,* **who shall do according to what is in My heart and mind.** *And I will build him a sure house, and he shall walk before My anointed forever. (emphasis mine)*

A faithful person speaks face to face with God.

Numbers 12:6-8 (KJV)

> *And he said, Hear now my words: If there be a prophet among*
> *you, I the Lord will make myself known unto him in a vision,*
> *and will speak unto him in a dream. My servant Moses is not*
> *so, who is **faithful** in all mine house. With him will I speak*
> *mouth to mouth, even apparently, and not in dark speeches,*
> *and the similitude of the Lord shall he behold: wherefore*
> *then were ye not afraid to speak against my **servant** Moses.*
> *(emphasis mine)*

Favour comes on the faithful, positioning them for rulership, because they devotedly execute what is on the heart and mind of the Lord. This is true sonship as Jesus noted in John 5:19,

> *So Jesus answered them by saying, I assure you, most*
> *solemnly I tell you, the Son is able to do nothing of Himself*
> *(of His own accord); but He is able to do only what He sees*
> *the Father doing, for whatever the Father does is what the*
> *Son does in the same way [In His turn].*

Scripture shows that governance is given to the faithful. It is remarkable to note with regards to His kingdom that the higher we are promoted, the greater servants we become. Jesus told His audience in Matthew 23:11, the greatest among them would become their servant, for to lead is to serve. The verses below expose a direct correlation between faithfulness in God's house and being promoted to rule over the Lord's possessions (sonship).

Luke 12:40-44

> *You must also be ready, for the Son of Man is coming at an*
> *hour and a moment when you do not anticipate it. Peter said,*

*Lord, are You telling this parable for us, or for all alike? And the Lord said, Who, then is that **faithful steward**, the wise man whom his master will set over those in his household service to supply them their allowance of food at the appointed time? Blessed (happy and to be envied) is that servant whom his master finds so doing when he arrives. Truly I tell you, **he will set him in charge over all his possessions.** (emphasis mine)*

Nehemiah 7:2

*I gave my brother Hanani, with Hananiah the ruler of the castle, **charge** over Jerusalem, for Hananaiah was a more **faithful** and God-fearing man than many. (emphasis mine)*

Nehemiah 13:13 (KJV)

*And I made treasurers over the treasuries, Shelemiah the priest, and Zadok the scribe, and of the Levites, Pedaiah: and next to them was Hanan the son of Zaccur, the son of Mattaniah, for they were counted **faithful** and their office was to distribute unto their brethren. (emphasis mine)*

1 Corinthians 4:1-2

*So then, let us [apostles] be looked upon as ministering servants of Christ and stewards (trustees) of the mysteries (the secret purposes) of God. Moreover it is [essentially] required of stewards, that a man should be found **faithful**, [proving himself worthy of trust]. (emphasis mine)*

Faithful With Another Man's — God Will Give You Your Own

Luke 16:12 (NKJV)

And if you have not been faithful in what is another man's, who will give you what is your own?

The story of Elijah and Elisha (1 Kings 19, 2 Kings 2) perfectly depicts faithfulness as a fundamental factor in preparation for governance.

When Elijah ran for his life in fear of Jezebel, he came to a cave and hid. The Lord spoke to him there and instructed him to anoint Elisha in his place. Elijah obeyed the Lord and found Elisha ploughing oxen in the field.

1 Kings 19:19-21 (NKJV)

So he departed from there, and found Elisha the son of Shaphat, who was plowing with twelve yoke of oxen before him, and he was with the twelfth. Then Elijah passed by him and threw his mantle on him. And he left the oxen and ran after Elijah, and said, "Please let me kiss my father and my mother, and then I will follow you." And he said to him, "Go back again, for what have I done to you?" So Elisha turned back from him, and took a yoke of oxen and slaughtered them and boiled their flesh, using the oxen's equipment, and gave it to the people, and they ate. ***Then he arose and followed Elijah, and became his servant****. (emphasis mine)*

There are some relevant points to highlight in the way Elisha was called by God.

Elisha did not choose Elijah and Elijah did not choose Elisha. God chose Elisha to be Elijah's successor. This is also the case with us. God will choose who we need to mentor or be mentored by, to learn under and faithfully serve, not us. We often want to pick the person we learn from and serve under, and when this is the case it bears minimal fruit in our lives. The Lord is the one who chooses your Elijah, and you may not always be happy with His choice, but we need to understand that God knows best what we need to develop and become successful in our callings. Elijah would not have been an easy man to serve under, however, Elisha understanding the weight of what took place in Elijah throwing his mantle on him, immediately ran after Elijah. Elisha demonstrated honour when he was called by God and immediately followed Elijah. The only request he had was to say "goodbye" to his mother and father. He knew that following God's call would cause him to give up his life and say goodbye to everything he had, his parents included. He did not hesitate in counting the cost, but immediately left his livelihood to be faithful to the call of God.

Elisha was ploughing twelve oxen, and was with the twelfth when Elijah threw his mantle on him. As discussed previously in earlier chapters, twelve is the number of divine government. This was prophetically indicating that the Lord was calling Elisha into a governmental role.

Elisha did not immediately step into the position of governance that God had called him to as Elijah's successor, but rather he *served* Elijah faithfully for several years after that. Even though the Lord had called him and Elijah's mantle had been cast upon him as a demonstration of successorship, he still had to be trained in order to step into that call in due time. We need to also understand this. I have often heard people receive prophesies revealing the calling of God on their lives and they consequently assume that they will step into the fullness of their mantle straight away. This is not the case, because the Lord first requires faithfulness in what is another man's (faithfully serve another minister who is already walking in his/her calling), so you will be faithful in what is yours.

Elisha was faithful until the appointed time of Elijah's departure. He didn't get distracted by other projects, but was focused on fulfilling what God had asked of him which was to serve Elijah until he was no more. Elisha was pressured to leave Elijah in the last moments of Elijah's days on earth and Elijah even told Elisha to stay behind when he was going to the place over the Jordan to be caught up by the Lord. However, Elisha refused to leave Elijah because his focus and purpose were fixed. Elijah, furthermore, asked Elisha what he could do for him before departing and Elisha requested a double portion anointing of Elijah's mantle. Elijah promised Elisha that if he witnessed Elijah being caught up, his request would be granted (2 Kings 2). As the story unfolds, Elisha remained faithful until the end and saw Elijah being caught up to heaven in a chariot of fire.

We could encounter the same type of pressure that Elisha faced, in our seasons of servitude. Temptations could persuade us to finish the course early and promote ourselves before our time. People could give us advice that steers us away from reaping our inheritance, because they don't have the eyes to see or the faith for the process. Elisha received the inheritance of a double portion by staying the distance to see his master caught up. This prophetic picture depicts faithfulness as "seeing" a season to the end. The person we may be serving might not yet go to glory when the season shifts, but you will both know when the time for your promotion arrives.

Elisha was known as Elijah's servant which gave his ministry credibility.

2 Kings 3:11-12 (NKJV)

> *But Jehoshaphat said, "Is there no prophet of the Lord here, that we may inquire of the Lord by him?" So one of the servants of the king of Israel answered and said, "Elisha the son of Shaphat is here,* **who poured water on the hands of Elijah**. *And Jehoshaphat said,* **"The word of the Lord is with him***." So the king of Israel and Jehoshaphat and the king of Edom went down to him. (emphasis mine)*

The servant did not inform the king of Israel about the time when Elisha parted the Jordan by striking it with his mantle, or when Elisha healed the waters that caused barrenness among the people, nor did he speak of the time when a bear ate the boys who mocked Elisha. A reputation of miracles did not validate him as a man who could hear God. No, Jehoshaphat was only informed that Elisha poured water on Elijah's hands which was enough for the king to discern that the *word of the Lord was with him*. It was his faithful service unto the man of God that validated Elisha's ministry.

One thing to take note of concerning Elisha's training were his duties of service to Elijah which were not prophetic in nature. *Elisha poured water on Elijah's hands*. This doesn't sound too spiritual does it? I would say it was a very practical and natural service to the man of God which is often how service and training look like. These days, however, some might assume that mentorship consists of hours and hours of teaching, counselling and serving the student. On the contrary, biblical mentorship looks quite different. Elisha received the prophet's reward by sowing service unto Elijah. He reaped the anointing that was on Elijah's life by faithfully attending to his needs, not by sitting and listening hours to him. Obviously, by walking alongside Elijah on a daily basis, Elisha would have learnt about the prophetic realm and what it meant to be a prophet. Nevertheless, the paradigm of mentorship is service-oriented.

A lot of our tasks in our training periods might seem irrelevant to the final outcome of what we are called to. In my early years of ministry training, I was assigned to the role of "girl Friday" within the ministry. I was elated that I had some place to serve and be a part of all God was doing. I would run errands, pick up dry cleaning for the pastoral staff, buy their lunches, pick up the postage, drive travelling ministers to and from the airports, and tonnes of other "natural" tasks. Even after I had completed ministry training school, these still remained my tasks. Yes, I was promoted with other assignments within the ministry and was given more responsibility as I was proven faithful, but I was not given the pulpit straight away just because I had a calling on my life that incorporated preaching and teaching; there would come a due time for that promotion. To assume that someone should share their pulpit with you shows arrogance and entitlement. Many who are in training expect their mentors to share the platform with them or give them all types of ministry titles and positions, but we must remember that God is the one who promotes in due time.

1 Peter 5:6-7 (NKJV)

> *Therefore humble yourselves under the mighty hand of God, that He may exalt you in due time, casting all your care upon Him, for He cares for you.*

People often ask me, "Do you mentor?" or "Will you mentor me?" What they are asking is this, "Can you just pour into me all you have learnt and answer all the questions I have and be there whenever I need someone to counsel me, run over stuff with, pray for me when I am troubled or need help?" etc., etc., etc. They don't understand that true mentorship is serving your mentor and not the other way around.

I mentor the Body of Christ through my writings and teachings, and I enjoy equipping, and building up, teaching and establishing people into maturity, but that is what I do on a corporate level. God handpicks those for me to mentor privately, and brings them to me as part of our ministry even if it is from the other side of the world. I don't choose them and they don't choose me. God puts it in people's hearts to serve a mentor. Very few that come to our ministry I mentor at an Elisha level, it all depends on the leading of God and His perfect will. Others may come to our ministry to serve other leaders within our ministry. God has handpicked them to be Elijahs and Elishas. Ultimately, if God has brought you to a place, allow Him to choose your Elijah, and just have an attitude to serve, rather than receive. In this space, believe me, you will receive like Elisha double fold return on the service you have shown. It is God who brings the increase, He pours out on your life, so trust His judgement, His way and His timing in all your seasons, and you will surely arrive where you need to be when you need to be there.

We must all apprehend that we cannot skip the servant stage in our training and preparation, regardless of our callings or ranks in the kingdom. You may wish to be mentored by a specific person, but God might pick someone else more suitable for you. You need to trust God's choice, because the vessel He chooses for you to serve and learn from, holds significant keys and the experiences and lessons learnt from serving them are needed for your calling.

Not all lessons are enjoyable. God might choose an Elijah for you that grates your nerves. You may disagree with how they operate and become frustrated with their ways of doing things, but possibly God is needing to establish humility and honour in your life by serving them, because without those traits it is impossible to govern successfully in the kingdom. The Lord could have us serve under people who in our opinion cannot "see" our full potential and therefore seemingly hinder us in our capacity to grow in ministry. This is all development of character: learning to allow God to promote you and trusting that He will open the eyes of those who need to see you when they need to see you.

No one has the ability to hold us back from our calling. Only we do. We can abort our seasons by trying to run ahead and promote ourselves or we can quit because we think the season is taking too long. It is normally before a promotion that we are tempted to quit, like Elisha who heard voices trying to distract him from finishing his full course. Only you can hold yourself back, not any leader or person.

If you believe that you need a person to help you fulfil your calling then you will also believe that a person can hold you back from fulfilling your calling, which is a wrong paradigm of believing.

If this were the case then Joseph's brothers would have been able to hinder Joseph's dreams from coming to pass. Their betrayal nearly cost him his life, but God was in charge, not man. Only Joseph had the capacity to hinder his calling. He could have allowed despair to overtake him and become an unfaithful servant to Potiphar, but instead he was found faithful and served

Potiphar with an honourable heart. He could have also become bitter and angry with God for allowing his brothers to sell him into slavery and for letting Potiphar's wife accuse him of indecency which put him in prison for a crime he did not commit.

But no, Joseph was faithful in prison and was promoted even in jail. All odds were against Joseph's dream coming to pass and if man could hinder destinies then surely Joseph would not have succeeded. However, God upheld His promise to him and in due time Joseph was released from prison and positioned in his destiny. God has set your release date and we need to remember that He knows the times and seasons. Joseph's calling wasn't needed until the appointed season had come. You have a season and you are being prepared for that season. Loyalty and character are tested in these times, that is why the Lord would have you serve another man before He can give you your own. He tests your integrity and attitudes in even unjust situations.

We might think that someone is holding us back from promotion or from exercising more influence and responsibility etc., but if you are sure that God brought you where you are and you are meant to be there, then yield to God and allow the fullness of the season to develop you, so you will lack nothing as James 1:4 says.

I have learnt that people often want to jump on your bandwagon. They just want to use you as leverage to promote their ministry or get to where they need to be. Somehow they believe that they are entitled to be given opportunities within your platform or sphere of influence. I never take for granted an opportunity (small or large) that another minister gives me to serve God's people, either behind their pulpit or on their platform. It is an honour as I understand the price they have paid for God to give them that space. Everywhere I minister I thank those who have invited me, for allowing me the privilege to serve within a space they have developed with the Lord.

The Bible instructs us to be humble and unassuming, not to announce ourselves but to wait for someone to invite us to honourable places.

Luke 14:8-11 (NKJV)

> *When you are invited by anyone to a wedding feast, do not sit down in the best place, lest one more honourable than you be invited by him; and he who invited you and him come and say to you, "give place to this man," and then you begin with shame to take the lowest place. But when you are invited, go and **sit down in the lowest place**, so that when he who invited you comes he may say to you, "Friend, go up higher." Then you will have glory in the presence of those who sit at the table with you. **For whoever exalts himself will be humbled,** and he who **humbles himself will be exalted**."*

Anyone with an entitlement mentality is a massive red flag for me, because it reveals immaturity of character whereas humility is maturity. Sometimes people come into our ministry and say I am a worship leader and have played with Hillsong, or other large renowned ministries, believing that will impress and persuade me to give them a position or place them on the worship team. But what I have learnt over many years is that God is the one who promotes and puts people in positions. These days I purpose not to judge by what I see or hear at face value, as discussed in the fear of the Lord chapter, but to seek God's leading and guidance with respect to selecting and positioning people in our ministry and the timing of it all.

This is key to maintaining purity and unity within the ministry. In the past I tried to build things quickly by placing people in positions prematurely or purely by gifting which never bore good fruit only dissention, contention and competition. People who are assigned to positions prematurely lack honour in the areas where their faithfulness was not tested through serving. I have had to learn this the hard way. Now I wait on God and if I have to function on a skeleton crew to maintain unity and purity, I will.

Characteristics Of The Unfaithful

The Lord is not an irresponsible father who gives promotions to unfaithful people, because they not only hurt themselves but others too.

Luke 12:45-46

> *But if that servant says in his heart, My master is late in coming, and begins to strike the menservants and the maids and to eat and drink and get drunk, The master of that servant will come on a day when he does not expect him and at an hour of which he does not know, and will punish him and cut him off and assign his lot with the unfaithful.*

The servant's service here was conditional. He temporarily did what was required of him and quickly displayed unfaithful leadership after a while. If certain areas in our heart are impure, it might go well for some time, but when circumstances don't go according to plan we could lose the plot. Are we going to be steadfast and show trustworthiness (faithfulness) so God can rely on us to not yield under pressure, resort to carnal means, act in the flesh and hurt or damage the work of God.

You can find below the example of the Israelites' unfaithfulness in the wilderness.

Exodus 32:1

> *When the people saw that Moses delayed to come down from the mountain, [they] gathered together to Aaron, and said to him, Up, make us gods to go before us; as for this Moses, the man who brought us up out of the Land of Egypt, we do not know what has become of him.*

They obviously weren't *convinced* or steadfast in their waiting. Waiting can be the greatest purifier of our motives. I once heard someone say TIME is like a poultice, it draws out the impurities of the heart.

The question we need to ask ourselves is this, "When things don't happen in our timing, or understanding, are we going to continue in what the Lord has last said?

Luke 16:10 (KJV)

> *He that is faithful in that which is least is faithful also in much: and he that is **unjust** in the least is unjust also in much. (emphasis mine)*

This verse reveals that unfaithful people are *untrustworthy* and *unjust* leaders.

According to Strong's concordance, the Greek meaning for the word *unjust* is: treacherous, wicked, **unrighteousness according to a heathen standard.**[77] (emphasis mine)

To be faithful means to continue in God's way of doing things and not resorting to a heathen standard which is what the children of Israel did when they turned to idolatry. When things don't work out according to our plans or doing it God's way didn't turn out as we had envisioned, will we resort to doing it our way or the world's? Will we continue in the way God has outlined in His Word? I'm sure the *way* Joseph arrived at his destiny was not the way he had imagined. However, despite multiple injustices, he didn't forsake his belief in God and kept his standard of integrity without lowering it due to wicked plots of betrayal and accusation that were playing out around him. This was Joseph's test of faithfulness which he passed by staying true to integrity and God's way. Experiencing injustice

---

77   James Strong. Strong's Expanded Exhaustive Concordance of the Bible
        (Nashville: Thomas Nelson, 2009), s.v *"unjust"*

can sometimes test our hearts. Will we forgive, love our enemies and honour our leaders even when they do us wrong? These circumstances are all there to test the faithfulness of our hearts, whether we would yield under a heathen standard or respond according to the standard of God's Word.

Luke 16:10-12 teaches us that how we behave in the small, insignificant things is how we will act in more important things. Will we choose integrity in the little? If you choose the heathen path in the little, you will take that path also in the large. You won't execute what's on the heart and mind of God, which is His written Word.

Another sign of an unfaithful person who should not be trusted with positions of authority is *gossip*.

Proverbs 11:13 (KJV)

> *A talebearer revealeth secrets: but he that is of a faithful*
> *spirit concealeth the matter.*

One thing I have learned in life is that if someone is talking to you about someone else, be sure they will talk about you to others. I don't trust people who tell tales and I discern immediately that they are untrustworthy and unfaithful.

A GOSSIPER is unfaithful and lacks integrity (trustworthiness) which is part of being faithful.

In our ministry we will never promote a backbiter, slanderer, a person who undermines authority, a gossip or a talebearer, because these traits reveal the heart.

They will turn on you and betray you as soon as they get offended. Will I stop loving them? No. I will still show them unconditional love. You might think that's fake. No, it is not. Trust is different from love. I will continue to be kind to them and honour them, I just won't trust them or share with them the secrets of my heart. God is calling a people He not only loves but trusts. These are the ones He announces as faithful at the end of the age.

The Reward Of The Faithful

If God is truly the Lord of your life, then you can rest assured He has your best interests at heart. He desires to see you become all He has purposed for you. He sees the end from the beginning and we must position ourselves under His mighty hand, allowing Him to take us where we need to be and when we need to be there. Remember that the grass isn't greener on the other side of the road. Stop looking for ways out of the process and a better "option" that benefits YOU. Allow God to refine and develop you into a faithful person who serves HIS interests, NOT YOUR OWN, so you may hear His beautiful words, *"Well done though good and faithful servant enter my rest."*

Matthew 25:23

> *His master said to him, Well done, you upright (honourable, admirable) and faithful servant! You have been faithful and trustworthy over a little; I will put you in charge of much. Enter into and share the joy (the delight, the blessedness) which your master enjoys.*

It is FAITHFULNESS that is rewarded at the end of the age. The Lord doesn't say here, "Well done you most talented and gifted person!" There will be many highly gifted and talented people that will not hear these words, because the reward is reserved for those who have shown loyalty and allegiance to His ways and Word. They are the ones He will entrust with rulership over all His possessions.

The *rest* is the reward. This is also the case in our seasons of life. If we strive for position or promotion then we will have to strive to maintain that increase, and will find ourselves surely burning out, because our characters are not developed enough to cope with the demand or the required level of maturity.

However, if we have allowed the Lord to develop our characters by faithfully serving another, through the good and the bad, through the comfortable and uncomfortable, then when promotion comes we will operate in the *rest* of God. In other words, *by His Spirit*, not our own efforts.

The position God has for you in His kingdom cannot be fulfilled by your gifting and talents alone. You will need Godly character that has been forged through fire and testing, to enable you to finish your race successfully.

You don't want to be a shooting star, but an enduring light in the dark hour.

Chapter 10:

HERE COME THE SONS

In my book "The Avenger - The Rise of the Kingdom", I share a vision I had in intercession more than 22 years ago regarding the coming forth of the sons of God. I felt led by the Lord to include it in this book as well.

The Last Wave – The Manifestation Of The Sons Of God

In 1999 in a time of intercession, I saw a vision of waves on the ocean. The Lord explained to me how He moves by His Spirit as waves of glory upon His body, which reveals different aspects of His person in order to "prepare" a people ready for the Lord. In this vision, I saw waves of different colours all representing different anointings and revelations of the Kingdom that were to be poured out upon His beloved in the coming years. There were waves of blue symbolising the prophetic move and waves of gold symbolising the glory. I then saw a wave of red which I knew was a wave of fire. Next I saw a wave of purple which I knew symbolised the miraculous. In this wave of the miraculous came the fear of the Lord, and as the Spirit of the Lord moved through His people in miracles causing the impossible to be made possible, a sense of great awe fell amongst the people.

Then I heard the Lord say to me,

"Look at this last wave, it will be the last wave of My Spirit upon the earth."

As I stood and looked, there was no wave rising on the ocean; it was dead calm. This suggested to me that this would be different somehow to the past waves or moves of God that I saw that come and then go. I saw the vast water dead calm. There was no movement nor suggestion of a coming and a going, but rather something that would remain. As I looked at the water, the reflection from the sun upon the water was blinding. I asked the Lord, *"What is this wave?"* Immediately I heard the scripture Psalm 37:6:

> *And He will make your uprightness and right standing with God **go forth as the light**, and your justice and right as the **[shining sun of] the noonday.** (emphasis added)*

This last wave I saw in the vision is what I believe all creation is groaning and crying out for. This is the manifestation or the "revealing" of the sons of God, His glorious bride radiating the reflection of the Son of Righteousness shining as the "noonday" sun. Note that noon is at twelve o'clock. Twelve signifies divine government. This last wave is the glory of the Lord upon His people walking in the divine government of heaven. This is where heaven meets earth through the sons of God. Righteousness and justice will be the mark of this Kingdom Government, and it will bring alignment and order to the chaos and rebellion on this earth. This government will subdue and rule in justice and righteousness, causing wrongs to be made right and that which is lawless to be in subjection to the authority of the Lord Jesus Christ.

Malachi 4:2 explains that the Sun of Righteousness will arise on His people with healing in His wings and His beams, causing them to be released like calves released from the stall leaping for joy. Then verse 3 explains the direct result of this move upon His people,

> *You shall tread down the lawless and wicked, for they shall be ashes under the soles of your feet in that day I shall do this, says the Lord of hosts.*

Notice here *who* signs off on this declaration. He signs off as the "Lord of Hosts". That is the King of Glory, the Avenger, as we read in Psalm 24. This speaks of the rule of Kingdom Government on the earth *through* His people. A people first avenged by the Lord, healed and set free (Malachi 4:2) then released to set others free (*tread down the lawless and the wicked becoming ashes under the soles of their feet*) (verse 3).

When the KING OF GLORY comes in, He not only shows Himself strong on behalf of His people, but He causes His Kingdom to operate *through* His people.

I believe, therefore, it is an urgent hour in which the people of God stand to prepare themselves for the days at hand. As we have discovered throughout the pages of this book, stepping into sonship is truly where dominion flows, it is operating *in His likeness* and *by His Spirit.*

Governed By God's Standards

Throughout the Epistles of the New Testament, Paul repeatedly expounds on the difference between spiritual maturity and immaturity. In 1 Corinthians 3, he notes that the brethren could not be spoken to as spiritual people, but as babes in Christ, because of their carnal ways. Spiritual maturity according to Romans 8 is the ability to be led by the Spirit of God and yield one's mind to things that gratify the Holy Spirit instead of the flesh. Those who walk in spiritual maturity are called sons of God. Sonship is the highest rank in the kingdom. We progress from children to servants and then from servants to sons.

John Bevere explains the difference between children of God and sons of God. He clarifies that the word 'son' used anywhere in the New Testament originates from either one of the two Greek words: *teknon* and *huios*. *Teknon* is used when describing a son by mere birth whereas *huios* refers to "one who can be identified as a son because he displays the character or characteristics of his parents". So to put it simply, the Greek word *teknon* means "babies or immature sons," while the Greek word *huios* is most often used to signify "mature sons".[78] Romans 8:14 (NKJV), *For as many as are led by the Spirit of God, these are the sons [huios] of God,* suggests therefore, that the mature sons are the ones led by His Spirit. "Sons" have been chastened by the Lord (Hebrews 12:5-11) and have learnt submission to authority. They are not governed by this natural realm, but by the Law of God written on their hearts. The Word of God is their standard and they have laid themselves as living sacrifices, holy and acceptable unto the Lord.

Romans 12:1-2 (NKJV)

> *I beseech you therefore, brethren, by the mercies of God, that you present your bodies a living sacrifice, holy, acceptable to God, which is your reasonable service. And do not be conformed to this world, but be transformed by the renewing of your mind, that you may prove what is that good and acceptable and perfect will of God.*

Offering your life as a living sacrifice is a dedication unto the Lord. When God's people live for Him, they will be consumed by Him. Fire consumed the sacrifices on the altars in the Old Testament, as a display of God's pleasure and acceptance of the sacrifice. Hebrews 12:29 says that God is indeed an

---

78   John Bevere, "When Should I Leave My Church?", ministrytodaymag.com, August 4, 2013, www.ministrytodaymag.com/leadership/calling/20008-john-bevere-when-should-i-leave-my-church

all-consuming fire. When we lay our lives down for the Lord and are consumed by His fire, we operate in overcoming power, as described in Malachi 4:3,

> *And you shall tread down the lawless and the wicked and they shall be ashes under the soles of your feet in the day that I shall do this, says the Lord of Hosts.*

What causes ashes? The correct answer would be fire. So people "treading down" and walking in dominion and governmental power, leaving the enemy as ashes under their feet, speaks of a people who have laid down their lives as a living sacrifice and are walking in the very presence of God Himself.

They are not conformed to this world, neither do they adapt themselves to customs or ideals, but are transformed by God's Word and His standard of righteousness is their governing blueprint. A person's image is fashioned and molded by whatever they conform to.

Conform: to act in accordance to prevailing standards and customs, to be obedient or compliant, **to be similar or identical.**[79]

Those who act according to the world's standards, will look identical to them. However, those who conform to the Word of God, will be *transformed* into the image of Jesus, the Son of God.

Jesus was the patterned Son, as He is, so are we in this world (1 John 4:17). Jesus as a son reflected the face of His Father (John 14:9). As God's people conform to His standards of the Word, they will walk as sons on this earth and as Jesus did, govern according to the Father's will in heaven.

---

79   Merriam – webster.com, conform, www.merriam-webster.com/dictionary/conform., accessed 4/02/21

A Governing People Governed By Love

People will govern by what governs them. If God's people are governed by His standards, love will be present.

Matthew 24:12

> And the love of the great body of people will grow cold **because** of the multiplied lawlessness and iniquity. (emphasis mine)

Notice here the love of people grow cold *because of* multiplied lawlessness. To rephrase it, love grows cold where no standards are upheld. Lawlessness means without law and iniquity is wilful disobedience.[80] People who are governed by self-centeredness without restraint are unable to love and walk by faith.

Galatians 5:6 (NKJV)

> For in Christ Jesus neither circumcision nor uncircumcision avails anything, but faith working through love.

Faith that works by love is what overcomes. So love is required in order to overcome and for love to be present, believers must be conformed to God's standards instead of being a law unto themselves. God's standards involve laying down one's life for the brethren. It also includes the saints loving the Lord their God with all their hearts and denying themselves to follow and obey Him (John 14:15).

Love is truth, it is not watering down God's standards to please and appease. His standards of truth bring freedom and victory for humanity (John 8:32).

---

80   What is the difference between sin, iniquity and transgression, gotquestions.org, January 2 2020, www.gotquestions.org/iniquity-sin-transgression.html

The enemy, on the other hand, seeks to disempower God's people by deceiving them into believing that true freedom equals no standards. Lawlessness, therefore, is a recipe for bondage. A generation bound in lawlessness is bound in darkness.

When God's people are ruled by the world's definition of love, their view of God is incorrect and obscure. Some new age concepts express that love has no boundaries, which is heresy and clearly deviates from the Word of God. Some believe that God's love is a license to act as they please, assuming that God understands their hearts.

Which husband on earth would approve the love of his life going out each night to act as a whore? If he would consent to it, he is not in love.

The Lord is a jealous lover (Exodus 20:5), He is jealous over our affection. His love sent Him to the cross, causing Him to endure a horrific death. God's people sometimes have double standards, they expect loyalty from their spouses, but think the Lord has lower standards with them. Modern world philosophies call tolerance for evil love, which is wrong. This earthly concept of love causes people to be out of balance and not walk by faith.

God's people are perfected and *matured* in love (1 John 4:18). This love speaks of redemption to the lost in contrast to contamination which indicates weakness.

Sons Of Light

The sons of God have fellowship with one another by walking in the light as He is in the light (1 John 1:7). Those who partner with hatred, judgements, bitterness and offence only add to the darkness they are supposed to be invading. God's people are called to be agents of light breaking through the darkness, which involves having fellowship with another. Jesus said in John 13:35 that the world will recognise His disciples because of their love for one another, meaning that the world will perceive WHO they follow because of their love.

To walk in the light means to stand out, be different and peculiar. Isaiah 60 says that to that light, kings and nations will come. Those seeking the truth will be drawn to it, but those who love darkness will be repelled by it. The spirit of truth makes people walk in the light. His Word is a lamp unto our feet and a light unto our path (Psalm 119:105). The light of His Word of truth is the light for His people and if they are not walking according to His Word, they are living in darkness.

The Answer To Darkness Is Not More Darkness
The Answer To Darkness Is Light

It is not for the church to water down and compromise the Word of God in order to save the world. On the contrary, they are called to be a beacon of hope to those in despair and disheartenment caused by darkness.

The earth is groaning, the sound is intensifying, all creation is calling for the sons of God to come forth. They will reflect the face of Father by denying themselves and loving one another. These God-fearing, covenant people who are surrendered in humility, will break through the darkness and call forth the dawn of the new day. In other words, they will bring forth the third day, the day of the Lord's power, resurrection, overcoming, ruling and reigning bride. They shall govern not by might, nor by power, but *by His Spirit*. In faith they will operate, led by the Spirit. As they *live for Him*, they will be *led by Him*. Let the Spirit and the bride say come! Come Lord Jesus, come!

CONCLUSION

May the Lord continue to unlock the mysteries of this era as His saints prepare themselves for the grand finale of the ages and fix their focus on the highest calling (to know Him intimately), forsaking all the pollution of the world that would distract and hinder that calling from being realised. As His people lay hold of this high calling to "know Him", they will apprehend and also become acquainted with the "power of His resurrection" and step into the Third Day, The Day of Ruach (Philippians 3:10).

This hour echoes the call to consecrate oneself as Joshua instructed the children of Israel before entering into the promised land, which prepared them to witness the display of the Lord's wonders (Joshua 3:5). The outpouring of the latter glory is upon the end time church, and time is of essence to stand ready.

As discussed in this book, the blueprint of covenantal governing sonship is comprised of covenant (consecration, obedience, allegiance, faith and faithfulness), walking in the fear of the Lord, humility and meekness. These elements are the core foundations to operating in the victorious governmental power that is set apart for the third day church.

It is vital His people have ears to hear, and eyes to see what the Spirit of the Lord is currently saying. May a surrendered heart and a listening ear be the fruit of repentance John the Baptist so boldly called for in preparing God's people for His coming. As the spirit of Elijah goes forth in this day, beckoning the saints to return to covenant, a faith-filled, kingdom subduing, overcoming people, who demonstrate the power of the kingdom will be established. It is time for the sons of God who know their inheritance and original governmental blueprint to come forth and reveal the face of Father to the earth. These ones will know how to function in their governmental birthright and release heaven's will on earth in *His likeness* and *by His Spirit*. All creation is waiting.

BIBLIOGRAPHY

Averback, Richard. "The Holy Spirit in the Hebrew Bible and Its Connections to the New Testament". Bible.org. 2 Feb 2009. www.bible.org/seriespage/1-holy-spirit-hebrew-bible-and-its-connections-new-testament

Bevere, John. Breaking Intimidation. Lake Mary, Florida: Charisma House, 1995

Bevere, John. The Fear of the Lord. Lake Mary, Florida: Charisma House, 1997

Bevere, John. Under Cover. Nashville, Tennessee: Thomas Nelson Inc, 2001

Bevere, John. "When should I leave my church?". Ministrytodaymag.com. August 4, 2013, www.ministrytodaymag.com/leadership/calling/20008-john-bevere-when-should-i-leave-my-church

Bock, Darrell L, Glaser, Mitch. "The meaning of Leaven in the Passover Seder". chosenpeople.com. Accessed 01/29/2020, https://www.chosenpeople.com/site/the-meaning-of-leaven-in-the-passover-seder/

Brown-Driver-Briggs Hebrew and English Lexicon. Clarendon Press, 1977

Clay Thompson, "Motherland or Fatherland? It all depends on culture", azcentral.com, February 10, 2015, www.google.com.au/amp/s/amp. azcentral.com/amp/23178367

Dictionary.com, s.v. "contumacious", Accessed November 30, 2020, https://www.dictionary.com/browse/contumacious

Dictionary.com, s.v "incredulous", Accessed November 30, 2020, https://www.dictionary.com/browse/incredulous?s=t

Johnson, Bill. When Heaven Invades Earth. Shippensburg, PA: Destiny Image Publishers, Inc. , 2003

Joyner, Rick. The Army Of The Dawn. South Carolina: Morning Star Publications Inc., 2015

Joyner, Rick. The Call. Charlotte, NC: Morning Star Publications, 1999.

Joyner, Rick. The Final Quest. Fort Mill, South Carolina: Morning Star Publications,1996.

Lexico.com, s.v. "endurance", Accessed 5/8/21, www.lexico.com/definition/ endurance

Lexico.com, s.v. "kingdom", Accessed 12/01/2020 www.lexico.com/ definition/kingdom

Lexico.com, s.v. "patience", Accessed 5/8/21, www.lexico.com/definition/ patience

Lexico.com, s.v "patriot", Accessed October 14, 2019, www.lexico.com/ definition/patriot

Lexico.com, s.v. "persistence", Accessed 5/8/21, www.lexico.com/definition/ persistence

Lexico.com, s.v "purge", Accessed July 19, 2021,www.lexico.com/definition/ purge.

Linsalata, Drew. "EP1010 – The Selfish Nature of Anxiety and Fear". theanxioustruth.com. March 25, 2020, https://theanxioustruth.com/selfish-anxiety/

Lucey, Candace. "What is the Meaning of Zion in the Bible?". Christianity. com. July 03, 2019. www.christianity.com/wiki/bible/what-is-the-meaning-of-zion-in-the-bible.html

"Meaning and origin of: Elizabeth". familyeducation.com, accessed 14 December 2020, www.familyeducation.com/baby-names/name-meaning/ elizabeth

"Meaning of numbers in the bible, the number 12". biblestudy.org, accessed 27 December 2020. www.biblestudy.org/bibleref/meaning-of-numbers-in-bible/12html

Merriam-Webster.com Dictionary, s.v. "revive", accessed November 10, 2020, www.merriam-webster.com/dictionary/revive.

Oliver, Robert. "How To Transport An Ark", clintonnc.com. March 2019, https://www.clintonnc.com/news/38232/how-to-transport-an-ark

Piper, John. "The New Covenant and the New Covenant People". Desiring God. org. February 7, 1993, www.desiringgod.org/messages/the-new-covenant-and-the-new-covenant-people

Rodriguez, Juan. "From Reed to Rock", the defender.org. accessed 01/29/2020, http://www.thedefender.org/From%20Reed%20to%20Rock.html

Strong, James. Strong's Expanded Exhaustive Concordance of the Bible. Nashville: Thomas Nelson, 2009

Sumrall, Dr. Lester. The Millennial Reign of Christ. Indiana: LeSEA Publishing, 2009. PDF

Thayer, Joseph. Thayer's Greek English Lexicon. Hendrickson Publishers, 1995

"The Former and Latter Rains in Israel". oneforisrael.org. May 27, 2016, www.oneforisrael.org/amp/bible-based-teaching-from-israel/the-former-latter-rains-in-israel

Vocabulary.com. Accessed 11/26/2020. www.vocabulary.com/dictionary/scepter

Vriezen, Th. C. "Ruach Yahweh (Elohim) in the Old Testament". Neotestamentica, Issue 1, Jan 1966:50-61.

"What is a Covenant? Biblical meaning and Importance today". Christianity. com. April 17, 2019, www.christianity.com/wiki/bible/what-is-a-covenant-biblical-meaning-and-importance-today.html

"What Is The Difference Between Sin, Iniquity And Transgression?". gotquestions.org. January 2 2020, www.gotquestions.org/iniquity-sin-transgression. html

What is the origin of the phrase 'Mother country'? phrases.org.uk, accessed October 14, 2019, www.phrases.org.uk/meanings/mothercountry

.

Printed in Great Britain
by Amazon

72367645R00122